Win that Pitch!

WIN THAT PITCH! . . .

. . . is a new business blueprint particularly for service firms. It is vital reading for all lawyers, accountants, marketing and management consultants, headhunters, PR firms, financial advisors, architects, surveyors, advertising agencies and all other service organisations.

Win that Pitch!

How to Secure

New Business

and Keep Clients

QUENTIN BELL

KOGAN
PAGE

DEDICATION

This book is dedicated to the successful new career of my mate Anthony Minden-Wilson, and his marketing director, Annie.

First published in 1993

Kogan Page Limited
120 Pentonville Road
London N1 9JN

British Library Cataloguing in Publication Data

A CIP record for this book is available from the British Library.

ISBN 0 7494 0905 3
    0 7494 0692 5 (Paperback)

Typeset by Photoprint, Torquay, Devon
Printed in England by Clays Ltd, St. Ives plc.

CONTENTS

ACKNOWLEDGEMENTS

Acknowledgements must go to all those long suffering clients that have in the past endured one of my pitches – but particularly to Francis Hallawell and Beverley Walker at QBO – and those pitch superstars that gave generously of their free time to be mentioned in this book.

INTRODUCTION

THE ROUND TRIP OF THE PITCH

This book is not about presentations, or how to present. It's about pitches, and how to pitch. And that is quite different.

'Presentational training' is, for me, a rather coy phrase. It's as if the mastery of how to present well to an audience is somehow detached from reality – a sort of academic exercise, if you like; a worthy pastime, like amateur dramatics.

But there's an absolutely vital element missing there – like a viper without venom, a lion without a roar, a shark without a bite. It's the winning element. For what's the purpose in presenting your ideas, if nobody is won over to your point of view? None. What's the point of presenting for new business, if you consistently lose? None.

Winning is the element that turns a presentation from being a rather twee, inward-looking affair, into an externally-focused, well-honed 'winning-machine'.

So, this book is all about how to oil, shine and polish your winning machine to maximum effect, and how to use it to win that new business pitch.

But it doesn't stop there with the new business caper, because the winning formula can be extended beyond this, to the radio and TV studio (we touch on how to win at interviews); the conference room (we take a glance at seminars and the like); and the ballroom (we consider some of the skills of the after-dinner speech). Although my main thrust is directed at how to cope with the traditional new business event, I extend the meaning of the word 'pitch' to embrace these other areas too.

And the commonality between them? All are connected via the

pitch, because as a business person you can master them to help increase your two most valuable commodities – your reputation, and as a result, your profit.

The book is directed primarily at service businesses: those fascinating, fast-moving businesses that have dominated the UK economy of late by doing what I believe the British do particularly well – selling their skills.

So if you need to sell *your* skills, whether these are creative or not so creative, and you're a law firm, accountancy practice, architect, headhunter, computer consultancy, chartered surveyor, direct marketing, sales promotion or design firm, management consultant, advertising agency, financial consultant or PR firm, or the like – then this book is for you, and I hope the following pages will help you win more pitches.

Most importantly, I hope it'll usefully guide you to the actual pitch in the first place: what's the point in sweating and preening in front of your bedroom mirror each night, if you haven't a clue how to convince an unsuspecting prospect that he or she should grant you an audience to begin with? None – unless you actually begin to fall in love with your nightly monologue.

The following pages will hopefully give you the lot: from identifying your prey and getting a foot in the new business door, through to mounting the pitch, and helping to keep the damned business when you win it. In short . . . the round trip of the pitch.

But you can't win them all, of course. I suppose over the last 20 years running The Quentin Bell Organisation – a 'top-ten' PR consultancy – I've been involved in hundreds and hundreds of new business pitches, but perhaps won only half of them.

I'm happy with that, because one simply can't legislate for everything, no matter how brilliant one is. For clients or customers will hate or love you instantly before you utter a word. Instinctively. Some will appoint a load of twits – they are the crowd known to you as your competitors – despite (as you groan afterwards to your colleagues) your pitch being more relevant and inspiring. And vice versa. There is simply no rhyme or reason to it.

But the point is that you have to be good enough to win half, because the likelihood is that you certainly *won't* without some of the techniques, inspiration and elbow-grease that I hope this book imparts.

If you can't bear to endure the full book, I've cunningly devised some methods which will enable you to pretend to your boss, colleague or partner that you have. There are Summaries at the tail-end of each chapter, and 'Fundamental Truths' (referred to as FTs) peppered throughout the text to highlight some of the key points. Then there are 'Top Tips for the Pitch' which, when used with the cross-references to other relevant parts of the book, will I hope become a useful and succinct 'refer-back-to' section for constant referral.

In addition, there are several 'Asides' that are mainly personal observations or anecdotes that I hope break up the text by adding a little piquancy to what might otherwise be simply an academic diatribe: remember, the one thing this book is *not* is classroom theory. It is a compendium of my real-life experiences gained over 25 years working in the highly competitive PR business, where pitching is an essential part of everyday life if one is to survive and grow.

Pitching is also damned good fun. In fact, I have no hesitation in saying that the new business pitch is the most exciting pastime of all. In what other way can you spend just a couple of hours which – if you win – will make you feel as good as if you've reached the summit of Everest? It beats free-fall parachuting, low flying or group sex as a neat means of getting your kicks, believe me (although I must admit to having no personal experience of any of those three . . .).

And remember, as a team effort that will knock into touch the finer attributes of rugby football, it's an activity you will not just enjoy: it'll also threaten to swell your bank account, as you win each new client. What could be better? Money and enjoyment – what a great combination!

You don't just have to take my word for it, to coin a phrase. Because I've consulted some of the best pitchers* in the business to gauge their views: within the text I demonstrate *their* 'winning ways', *their* 'tricks of the trade'. If you can't pick up something from the combined talents of people like PR star Peter Gummer, and advertising legends Winston Fletcher and Rupert Howell – then heaven help you.

Finally, I do hope you will enjoy the read. Business books don't have to be serious, in my view: indeed, serious points made entertainingly in books (as well as in pitches) can be more memorable, and often are. Taking entertainment seriously is the first, most important lesson to learn . . . .

---

* Throughout the book I refer to 'pitchers' and 'pitchees'. The first refers to the pitching company itself, and the second to the prospect being pitched to.

SETTING THE SCENE

PITCHING: THE WHEN, WHO, WHERE AND WHY

When I conducted my very first pitch I simply couldn't keep my mouth closed. What's worse, even though I now try to look back, I can't recall a single thing about it. It's a complete blank. Mind you, it was 48 years ago, so maybe I'm excused. How come? I was being born, that's how.

OK, maybe I'm pushing an analogy too far – but the point I'm trying to make is that the art of pitching isn't something rather ethereal that only happens to other people: it's an inherent skill lurking in all of us, whether we realise it or not. So it follows that all of us have the innate potential to be good at it!

So the very first Fundamental Truth (FT) to learn is this:

■■■■■■■■■■■■ **FT Number 1** ■■■■■■■■■■■■

Successful pitchers (those pitching) are not born that way. They are made. True – some people learn the techniques more quickly than others, but there is no one in the universe that cannot become at least a competent (by which I mean successful) performer and, contrary to popular opinion, these are not just the extroverts of this world.
■■

Think about it. In your daily life you're either inviting people to pitch to you (and sometimes they're doing it without invitation, when they catch you annoyingly unguarded on the phone), or you're pitching to others.

The art becomes apparent at around puberty, as boys and girls vie for each other's affections. Young marrieds do it when they pitch for a mortgage, or that new job. When you go into a car showroom, you expect the salesperson to cogently pitch the brand benefits of his franchise to you, over those of his competition. Or, when you clip a coupon to receive holiday brochures, you anticipate that the tour companies will pitch to you through the written word, hopefully expressing the 'added value' of their product over others.

And, then there's the media: politicians will appear on TV, seemingly all day and all night, silly sods – each with a valid viewpoint, but often one that is diametrically opposed to the other; newspaper and radio advertisements will alluringly pitch products and services to you, whether you need them or not – even if you might want them, which is different altogether.

And then, damn it – just when you thought you were in the tranquility of your home, with TV and radio relegated to the garden shed – your partner corners you to ask a very special favour . . . and if it's done well, how the heck can you refuse?

And finally, to cap it all, your boss is taken ill with nervous exhaustion, leaving you nervously exhausted, having to make *his* after-dinner speech to a trade association, followed by *his* seminar the next day to the sales force – and a requirement to head up *his* new business pitch to a major multinational at the weekend. Bang goes your golf and your tranquility all at once. How do you cope? I hope you'll find out in this book.

It's all to do with the pitch, and we can't duck it. So the question that I must ask you is – if it's inevitable, why not learn to master it? Why not learn, in particular, to give effective new business pitches?

Let's now examine the scale of the beast: the 'when, who, where and why' of the pitch.

WHEN DO WE PITCH?

Just think about the business-related pitches one might make in a year:

■ influencing potential prospects or peer groups at an industry seminar;
■ getting your points across on radio;
■ an after-dinner speech to opinion-formers;
■ and of course, those new business pitches.

And so pitches can take place in the ballroom, auditorium, conference room, the broadcasting studio or the board room – and that might be just on Monday . . . .

In all these cases (and we touch on them later) you're on show; how you *cope* will determine how others rate you – and if you're a business person, being highly rated is vital, especially if you're a spokesperson or ambassador for your organisation dealing with external audiences as well as internal ones. (Which is not to demean internal communications, but simply to recognise that they often have a more limited audience, in terms of numbers if not influence.)

WHO PITCHES?

Just think of the diversity:

- An executive search firm needs to convince a multinational prospect of its global capabilities.
- An accountancy and law practice, like the rest of us, needs new clients.
- A PR firm or advertising agency is up for review by its client: how does it retain the contract?

In all these cases, there is one common denominator: *you*. Or, to be precise, people, like me and you, all of us consumed by irrational human failings such as fear, pride, insecurity and, I believe, a deep-rooted quest to succeed (or at least not to fail, or be seen to fail by others, our peers).

And make no mistake about it – it's *you* that counts in all of this pitching caper. *You* are the magic ingredient. *You* will be the one to win the day (or not) . . . the one that other people (your potential new business prospect) will buy.

■■■■■■■■■■■■■■ FT Number 2 ■■■■■■■■■■■■■■

People buy people, not organisations. So remember, whilst the reputation of your company and the standard of your physical execution will influence a decision, it will be *you* (and your colleagues) that matter most in clinching the deal.
■■

The first thing you need to do is learn about yourself. It's vital that you learn a bit more about 'you', and appreciate (as we'll discuss later) that your personality must shine through that stiff and rigid framework you tend, by arrangement with fear, to adopt when pitching.

Why is it, I wonder, that ordinary, nice, relaxed people seize up like an engine without oil when faced with an audience? I'll tell you why, it's because:

- It *appears* unnatural – you are denied the normal interaction that takes place in a casual conversation between friends: it's you on one side of the auditorium and them – detached and remote, formal and unforgiving (and sometimes unsmiling) on the other.
- You dwell too much for your own good on the potential horrors before the event – because you have time to do so (most pitches or speeches are arranged weeks, if not months in advance). And all this anticipation builds up uncontrollably inside you, until you turn into jelly and border on becoming a jibbering idiot.

Or do you? We'll look at my confidence-inducing formula later.

WHERE DO YOU PITCH?

Most learned books on the subject of pitching are excellent. But most also, in my view, are significant for what they *omit* (and much of what they contain is conventional wisdom, but that's another matter). So what do they leave out?

One such omission relates to environment: where you pitch – in terms of both physical and emotional aspects. If you're pitching for some new business to two blokes in a small conference room, you are likely to adopt a more 'casual' approach to the occasion then when you're making it a Very Formal Event, such as I did when the Quentin Bell Organisation pitched in a theatre environment to 45 executives from BT (then British Telecom).

But it cuts deeper than that. Turning a negative question into a positive answer during – say – a radio interview on BBC Radio 4's aggressive *Today* programme will require a different approach and attitude to a casual chat about the chairman's new book on, say, the *John Dunn Show* on BBC Radio 2 (and I should know, because I've done just that).

And there again, an after-dinner speech to trade association members and their partners will require a different technique which –

as we'll learn – does not include endeavouring to replicate Jimmy Tarbuck or Jasper Carrott: the joke-teller.

ASIDE

Speakers invariably fall into the joke-rendering trap, because they desperately want the audience to tell them they are loved and admired, by engendering the responsive giggle that a normal conversation would bring and thus make them feel relaxed. But in reality only one in fifty people are good at joke-telling, because it's an art form that takes professionals years to master.

■■■■■■■■■■■ **FT Number 3** ■■■■■■■■■■■

And remember: people expect comedians to be funny and are thus prepared to laugh – even before they come on stage. In a pitch, the opposite is true – they *expect* you to be serious, or at least sensible.
■■■

So, don't try – unless wit comes naturally, although even then there is a great difference between wit, which relies on 'bouncing' off other people's comments, and the joke-telling of a stand-up comic.

But back to the environment: there are common principles that apply, in order to help you win that pitch – as we'll discuss in Chapter 5.

WHY PITCH?

It's a valid question. Why indeed? Why not just sit behind your desk, knock back a pint at the pub, or stay in bed? Why on earth manoeuvre yourself *wittingly* into a situation that will make you shiver in your long johns and burst into a sweat of surf-wave proportions?

What mad person would agree to pitch in front of 100 key employees at a conference, when they can put their points across in a company newsheet, or launch a flotilla of memos, hiding behind these bits of paper instead of risking face-to-face contact?

Memo man (or memo woman, but less so) may still exist, but he does his company and himself a great disservice – because he'll be less successful than the competitor in the office down the road who accepts that public appearances of all types are a fundamental part of the job specification. Politicians accept (if not relishing the fact) that communication is a basic part of their job – *so why not businesspeople?*

■ ■ ■ ■ ■ ■ ■ ■ ■ ■ ■ ■ ■ ■ **FT Number 4** ■ ■ ■ ■ ■ ■ ■ ■ ■ ■ ■ ■ ■ ■

If you're a 'boss', then speaking (ie pitching) in all its forms is not just an item of your job specification – it's the most vital part, a duty.
■ ■

In particular, all directors (as opposed to just managers) are company ambassadors by definition. This responsibility can manifest itself either on radio, in the press, or during a staff briefing. It's a director's duty, and their destiny, to be a 'front person'.

But many do not take up this challenge, and it is not just technology-led entrepreneurs in manufacturing enterprises, or accountants, that (because they believe they are psychologically unsuited) are the culprits. Weedy cowards, calling themselves 'creative or extrovort managers' – who make a profession of avoiding confrontation (like you and me) – can fail too.

Leadership responsibility mustn't be shirked. Why? Because having a leader – *one who is seen to be a leader* – is what all successful firms share in common – although as Gerald Ratner, ex-head of the jewellery chain, and others, will testify, leadership can have its dangers. But isn't that what makes it so thrilling and challenging?

ASIDE

I don't believe in the current fad for flat structures in companies, because they don't accord with that fundamental natural desire in some humans to rise above others and lead from the front. But nor do I believe in autocracy in its worst hierarchical form, because such autocrats are stupid: they don't appreciate the need to cajole, involve and motivate people 'below' them in order to make the organisation work effectively. I believe in the *curved structure*, that applies the best of both.

But let's get down to the nitty-gritty and answer the most important 'why' question we have just raised: why pitch for new business?

Here are two reasons, that are indisputable facts:

1. COMMUNICATING CHANGE

Businesses are not static, they are machines of constant change. Change has to be managed. The most effective way to communicate change – both within the organisation and externally – is not in writing only (that's for short-sighted cowards) but through the superb human being that is called You. In a pitch, in other words, and *in person*.

■■■■■■■■■■■■■■ **FT Number 5** ■■■■■■■■■■■■■■

Come out of the closet and discard purposefully that facade of Memo Man (or Woman) that is part of all of us. Accept that face-to-face contact will contribute to your business success.
■■■

Let's take an example or two.

- You wouldn't (or shouldn't) inform a workforce about a major restructuring just by letter - you'd *tell* them, as well, wouldn't you?
- You wouldn't, (or shouldn't) allow them to learn about a relocation by reading it first in the trade press. You'd tell them first, wouldn't you?
- You wouldn't (or shouldn't) conduct a new business pitch by simply sending a written proposal. You'd take them through it, wouldn't you?

ASIDE

Whenever I've done that in the past because some bureaucratic organisation has requested it, we've never won the business. Why? Because they never experienced the chemistry of human contact, or saw the whites of our eyes.

No, in all these cases above you'd communicate verbally, even if you *also* put it in writing. The bit you cannot duck is the verbal pitch. Not if you're clever.

But there's another aspect to all this: whilst the new business scenario is the most likely place for a physical pitch to take place, many businesspeople fail when it comes to applying the same technique to other areas. They again hide behind the memo. But they shouldn't.

■■■■■■■■■■■■■■ **FT Number 6** ■■■■■■■■■■■■■

You utilise the verbal pitch as a new business vehicle for your own ends – so why not utilise the radio or TV studio, conference room, banqueting room, or factory floor as well? The answer is that not only should you, you must. As I say almost *ad nauseum* (or should it be PR

nauseum?) in my book *The PR Business*, messages are for managing, so why not manage them using as many tactics as you possibly can?
■■

2. REPLACING THE LOSSES

Businesses win new business. That's how they survive. But they also lose business. It's a fact of life. So whilst you may appear to read only about those new business successes in the trade press, because they hit the headlines, don't forget that someone's gain is invariably another's loss. And it could be yours.

So, that being the case, successful companies (particularly service firms like advertising, sales promotions or PR agencies, and now increasingly accountants and lawyers) have to implement continuous new-business programmes in order to ensure there is always a potential new piece of business lurking on the horizon, ready to be converted. And it's this piece of potential new business coming into the organisation at the *top* that will take the place of one that will fall out through the *bottom* – as it inevitably and most assuredly will.

In other words, new business pitching is essential if a company is even to stand still, let alone grow. That's what makes learning the skill of pitching so vital. Because you're not simply in the business of survival – you're in the business of growth. And becoming a better-honed pitcher will help.

But there is a fifth question that as yet we haven't asked:

HOW?

By courting your prey, that's how. Because there is no point in learning how to pitch if you have no mechanism for creating the opportunity to pitch in the first place. In short, how to develop new business leads. And that's what we'll examine in Chapter 2.

WHAT HAVE WE LEARNT?

- That pitching can take place on the factory floor, in the ballroom or auditorium, conference room, broadcasting studio or board room (and some might say in the bedroom, too, but that's another saucy story).
- That people buy people, not organisations.
- That the pitch environment is important – the style and tone matter.
- That pitching is your duty as a boss – don't hide behind memos!
- That pitching in person must be extended from the new business pitch to all possible areas: radio, conference, etc.
- That you must resist being a 'witless' joker.
- That you need to pitch to communicate change in an organisation, and as a vital new business tool to replace the customers that you'll inevitably lose.

2 HOW TO SET THE VICTIM IN YOUR SIGHTS!

In which we learn:

- How to simply formulate a new business action plan.
- Why being famous directly affects your bottom line by bringing in new business.
- How to get on the shopping list.
- Why reputation is like an antique table.
- Why the pitch should start before the prospect knows it.
- Why $(2 + 3) - 1 =$ opportunity!
- How for only £1.20 a week you could bring in thousands of pounds of new business.
- Your introduction to how, by tuning into 'the Wavelength', you can turn an idea into cash.

Most businesspeople think that the best and sometimes only way to get new business is to 'be visible' as a likely pitcher when a potential client is on the look-out. In short, to manoeuvre their firm into a position where they're a pretty likely candidate for inclusion on the client's shopping list.

They'd be right. But the most successful organisations, in my view, are those that don't just sit back and – like some people – wait for the world to shuffle up to kiss their feet. They have a master action plan.

That proactive plan identifies, well in advance, the key executives and key organisations to be targeted – long before the poor dears realise what's afoot. And quite right, too!

It's weird, I know, to say it – but I've noticed that once I've proactively dedicated time and effort at getting such a plan up and running, I've won new business. Why weird? Because sometimes the new business lead comes from another direction entirely – not related directly to the plan. It's as if by merely 'thinking new business' I've psychologically attracted it. Weird indeed? Maybe – but wait until you hear about 'the Wavelength', later on in this chapter.

WHY FAME HAS A VALUE

Before we move on to the Wavelength, let's just pause a second to examine the issue of the shopping list again, because it's very important. I'm a firm believer in fame. And by that, I mean 'becoming famous'.

Why? Because there is no doubt that, whilst preparing their plans, many company marketing and PR departments glibly over-use phrases like wanting to become 'high-profile' and wanting to develop 'increased awareness'; being well known, nevertheless, does matter.

- Why else would autograph hunters queue up to record on a piece of used Kleenex the indecipherable scribble of some illiterate footballer?
- Why else would some businesspeople part with many thousands of pounds to hear Tom Peters, the management guru, speak pearls of wisdom?
- Why else are gossip columns in the tabloids so alluring?
- Why else has the royal family been so enduring for so long, despite its troubles and in defiance of rational explanation?

Answer: logic or rationality play no part in it. We all simply need – and demand – role models, whom we help 'make famous' as part of the process.

Put another way, it's because people want – need – to have these role models in order to associate themselves with the wise, rich . . . and famous. It's an emotional, irrational feeling that is a natural instinct in us all, to varying degrees. It has a value – often ignored – of its own.

My experience over the years has shown that consumers (that's you and me) are overwhelmingly more likely to buy famous, well-known branded goods (including supermarket own-brands), rather than lesser-known ones. And this is also true of the more up-market brands, which are more expensive: a high price can sometimes simply not be an issue if the product is 'famous' – witness Aston Martin, Christian Dior, Ray-Ban, *et al*.

And it's common sense, of course; again by arrangement with human nature. Why? Because whether they are expensive or cheap, we take comfort from people and things that are familiar, that are a known quantity to us, chiefly because, if questioned, we can mutter: 'Well, I chose them because of their reputation' and whether one views it as cowardly or not, hide behind that statement, especially if we're being challenged by an angry boss at the time.

This principle applies just as much to your mother choosing a breakfast cereal as it does to an office specifying, for example, a network of branded computers or automatic coffee machines. Someone once said, I believe, that 'No one was ever fired for choosing IBM', meaning that the purchaser is buying into (or hiding behind) this fine company's reputation (notwithstanding its recent difficulties and attempts through the 1990s to become more 'fleet of foot' in a changing market-place).

Why risk buying a less visible computer (even if it's cheaper) when you know that your boss, your financial director and you all share a common bond: a bond of faith in the reputation of your chosen supplier? You all know of them, trust them, and 'buy into their brand values'.

Some claim that the depression that hit the computer industry in the early 1990s – where identical technology available to all manufacturers turned brands into commodities – was a death knell. I doubt it: if a well-known brand comes out with a product as capable and as cheap as a more obscure make, I know which one I'd choose.

So, never underestimate the power of a good – and what's more, consistent – reputation. I should know, after all, because I've earned a living over the last 25 years or so in the PR business by carving, honing, building and managing the reputations of others.

■■■■■■■■■■■■■■ FT Number 7 ■■■■■■■■■■■■■

Being famous by building a reputation is essential if you are to become an exalted contender for the shopping list – and therefore run the risk of picking up the big contracts. Major firms don't buy what they perceive to be also-rans. They take comfort in, and sometimes hide behind, a suppliers' stated imagery.
■■

But wait. This is not to say that you have to be big to be famous: some specialist firms in a wide variety of industries are unheard of to you and me, but enjoy cherished reputations in their field.

Nor do I suggest that being famous *per se* is the key: as I point out in *The PR Business*, it's what you're famous *for* that matters – but that's another story.

But what I do say is that the reputation of a company, which builds up over a period of time, like layer upon layer of polish caringly applied to an antique table, is a most cherished asset – which is why big brand companies spend so much time and effort protecting their reputations.

ASIDE

When, in the spendthrift 1980s, QBO worked for Filofax, that company rightly waged a constant battle against their fine brand being viewed as a 'generic'. Every time, in other words, that a newspaper referred to 'Filofax' as a commodity, rather than a particular brand, they received a raspberry in the form of a legal letter from the organiser organisation. And quite right, too: Filofax was their unique and cherished brand name, built up over time, and was not to be applied generally to all organisers lest it undermined their unique and leading quality position in the market. What at the outset might appear to be an accolade (eg products like Hoover or Polaroid becoming a generic) is in fact a great threat, because consumers asking for – say – a Filofax in a shop run the risk of being served with a competitive make.

The major benefit of having a fine reputation as a powerful asset is not just to provide a warm glow for the employees and shareholders. It is the best, most practical lure to attract new business leads (although not necessarily clinching it, of course). It attracts leads like a Jaguar owner purportedly attracts gin and tonic.

Just as each new layer of polish on the antique table over time further protects the original wood and also provides a very special depth and patina, so too does the reputation of a company or organisation yield a very special individual shine, that is unique to them.

HOW TO FORMULATE A PROACTIVE NEW BUSINESS ACTION PLAN

So fame matters. But assuming you're already famous (and if you're not, you'd better hire a PR firm) then I recommend the next step is to formulate the proactive plan. To *make* things happen, not just wait for them to happen.

Here's one practical example of how you do it – and this applies to all service firms, all types, all sizes, all industries.

STEP ONE

Call all your executives together, having previously asked them to fill in a form that identifies all their past, personal, client industry experience (I'm assuming that there was life before they joined your firm). Get them to list individual companies within these specific industries.

STEP TWO

Prepare a list of your firm's current clients, and another that charts those you have worked for during the past five years, but have (ever so sadly) subsequently lost. And remember, too, there's no shame in losing business, because as sure as death and middle-age spread, it happens to all of us.

STEP THREE

Work up the following simple analysis on a flip chart, or similar, so that you identify:

1. Your current client portfolio and their industry sectors.
2. Those companies and industries in which your staff can claim to have gained past client experience – albeit elsewhere (and don't concern yourself with that – they're working for you now, damn it, so you're perfectly justified in claiming it as your own 'company corporate experience').
3. Clients/industries which your firm has been engaged in previously, but is no more.

Then make the following simple calculation before congratulating yourself on your astuteness and before passing round the peanuts: add 2 and 3 and then take 1 from it. Or, to put it in a psuedo mathematical manner, with a dash of flair added:

$$(2 + 3) - 1 = \text{opportunity!}$$

See what I'm driving at? If you're a headhunter, management consultant, law firm, accountancy practice, PR firm, advertising agency – or any other service firm where you feel your clients are concerned about you working for one of their competitors, then this formula is for you.

Why? Because what you'll be left with is a hit-list of potential market areas where you can claim experience but where there is no possibility of a conflict of interest. So go for it!

But how, do I hear you ask? Here's how:

1. Draw up your hit-list headings of potential industry sectors that the exercise reveals. These are hot targets where your firm is not currently represented and where no conflict with your current clients exists. For example, it may be:

— white goods (fridges, cookers);
— toiletries;
— brown goods (hi-fis, etc);
— travel and leisure;
— computers;
— drinks;
— healthcare.

2. If you don't already have a dedicated new business team (and don't fancy the expense of getting one up and running) hire a graduate trainee who is presentable, numerate and literate (if that's possible in one package) and call him (or her) your 'business development assistant' (or research assistant). That will buy you a lot for not too much money, because the graduate is likely to be just as keen to prove himself or herself in his/her first job, as you are on moulding him/her to your needs.

3. Charge the graduate with the task of researching all major companies in the sectors you've identified (above) as being non-competitive to your existing clients. How? Here's a suggestion that will cost you around £1.20 a week, but may offer the chance of winning thousands of pounds of business in return. Here's the little gem:

   — Subscribe to the selected industry's 'vertical' trade journal. ('Vertical is a term we use to describe media that cover the affairs of a specific industry or leisure interest group.) That'll not *just* give you the contact names – mentioned in various editorial articles that can be monitored over a period of time but – most importantly – reading the editorials will provide you with a proper 'feel' for a company and the industry environment in which it operates.

So, if you're a law firm wanting to attack the hotels market as a potential client source, then subscribe to – and assiduously monitor – *Hotel and Caterer* magazine or similar. Or, if you're a headhunting firm wanting to expand into the food retailing sector, buy – and read – *The Grocer* magazine or similar.

■■■■■■■■■■■■■ **FT Number 8** ■■■■■■■■■■■■■

The best way to ensure that a new business prospect will sit up and listen to you (as opposed to listening to one of your competitors) is to demonstrate that you possess a real feel for the issues and nuances affecting not just the prospect's company, but his industry as well'.

■■■

In a *Campaign* magazine survey published in 1992, it was revealed that 95 per cent of advertising agency clients rated 'understanding my product or service' as the best method of getting on a new business shortlist. Additionally, and in answer to the same question, 87 per cent of clients rated suppliers' maintaining regular contact as one of the best methods. (My own comparative survey follows towards the end of the book).

This is overwhelming evidence that getting a feel for a clients' business, and keeping in contact with the client, is vital. If you remember nothing else in this book, remember this and act upon it. And you can achieve this happy state of affairs quite simply, by reading the trade press. But most don't. Why? Because it takes time and trouble. But, if you're serious about increasing your customer base, why should this be an obstacle?

What we did at QBO, operating in the marketing services sector, was to scan each issue of the weekly marketing trade press – both for names of marketing directors and managing directors (our target personnel) written up in articles, and also for the content of the stories themselves. These were summarised and filed alongside copy letters that went to those prospects. Low tech? Yes. A computer database in sight? No. Effective? Yes!

That's one simple method to improve your hit list beyond recognition, and the most it will cost you is energy and time (and maybe £1.20 a week).

And, of course, it builds and builds, week by week, month on month, until you have quite a sizeable database that can allow you to begin a consistent dialogue with your prospects.

The pain and tedium of drawing up a target list of 100 or 1000 or so prospects is ameliorated when you win one of them: it makes the effort all worthwhile. And one decent client will probably pay for the entire investment as well . . . .

Your only problem? Keeping the list up to date, but this is hardly arduous because by continuing your consistent dialogue you'll do this as a matter of course.

There are other ways than reading the press, of course.

Here are two:

■ Contacting the trade association of your chosen target industry – their members' handbook will be a mine of information.
■ Prising background information out of colleagues, or hiring specialists who've worked in that industry before.

But, when it comes right down to it there is only one real key to winning new business – and it's so important it warrants an FT. Let me introduce you to the 'Wavelength'.

▪▪▪▪▪▪▪▪▪▪▪▪▪ **FT Number 9** ▪▪▪▪▪▪▪▪▪▪▪▪▪

New business is not something to be worked at spasmodically, or something just for the new business executive to deal with. It should permeate throughout the organisation all day, every day. Everyone in the organisation should be attuned to what I call the 'Wavelength'. This applies as much to the chairman as it does to the cleaner.

▪▪

ASIDE

An acquaintance of mine was hired by an established service firm to head their new-business thrust. It was a new appointment, but despite his skills and track record he was back on the street within months. Why? Because the outdated culture of the firms top brass hadn't grasped the significance of hiring a specialist. They didn't appreciate that they all had to contribute to the new business effort as a team, thinking naively instead that somehow the new bloke would do it all, like magic. They even denied my acquaintance access to the Chairman! Well, hopefully such nitwits will die out – because the truth is that the winning service firms of the 90s and beyond will be those that tune into the Wavelength.

It's amazing what information can be picked up by keeping your eyes and ears open. A comment on the radio news about an industry facing a potential legal problem should set the bells ringing at a law firm. But they have to be tuned not just to the radio, but to the 'Wavelength' in order to turn a casual remark into a formal opportunity – and then into cash.

Or maybe a newspaper item appears, charting the outdated management control of a major charity: this should alert management consultants to a real need. But are they on the Wavelength? If they are, then they'll be on to their charity sharpish; if not, the newspaper will be left on the 7.33am train to Waterloo with the rest. And so on.

LOOKING INWARDS FOR INSPIRATION

New business thinking can look inwards into the organisation for its stimulation, too. If an accountancy practice believes its own experience in a particular industry will benefit, say, advertising agencies by providing them with a simplified and more effective method of producing monthly management accounts to check their overheads and monitor their profits, then being attuned to the Wavelength will help them proactively sell that service to others – turning another idea into cash.

OK, so what exactly is the Wavelength? It's simply my name for a winning culture in an organisation. But it bears repeating again that it must permeate throughout that organisation, so that everyone is attuned to the new business possibilities that are buzzing around all the time ready and waiting – like butterflies to be netted.

In short, it's the culture of keeping ears to the ground, and eyes on the ball. (Have you ever tried keeping your ear to the ground with your eye on the ball as well? Note to myself: Maybe that's the wrong phrasing, but even contortionists should know what I mean.)

But here's the trick – how can you expect your executives to be attuned, if you haven't identified target industries for them to 'go after', to be receptive to?

Well, you've done so already haven't you, when you took 1 from 2 + 3 and discovered a treasure chest of opportunity for non-competitive, non-conflicting new business? Give them guidance – guidelines, a framework – and you'll begin to work wonders, believe me. But if you go after your new business with the attitude of a pair of sagging trousers, it'll fall away to the ground and won't work. Let's get some advice from an advertising guru whose new business trousers have *never* sagged.

THEIR WINNING WAYS: RUPERT HOWELL

This is an intermittent section of the book where we can share some of the secrets and experiences of the 'stars' of the pitching world (and I make no apologies for the fact that they come from the marketing services sector, for this area is where I believe the most experienced operators operate).

Rupert Howell, an old mate and our first star, has more qualifications than most: before starting his own highly successful ad agency (Howell Henry Chaldecott Lury) – he was Young and Rubicam's star new-business development director – so good that it justified Young and Rubicam giving him a Ferrari and mega salary to keep him. And his advice? Simply that New Business is different from Real Business. It's a simple statement, with massive ramifications. So, whilst everyone should be on my 'wavelength', to be totally successful an organisation must recognise that running their chosen profession requires skills that are totally different to those aimed at winning new business. As he says:

> When prospects come to see us it's not an advertising campaign they're initially after. They want to see us pitch to them – and the two disciplines require different skills and often different people.

But Rupert goes further:

> New business itself has to be further subdivided – because a New Business director whose skills require him or her to source new leads for the company, will have enough work to occupy working hours out of bed, restaurants and wine bars to have to delegate 'Business Development' to another. And the difference? Business development concentrates solely on increasing the levels of business from *existing* clients, as opposed to getting new ones [see Figure 1].

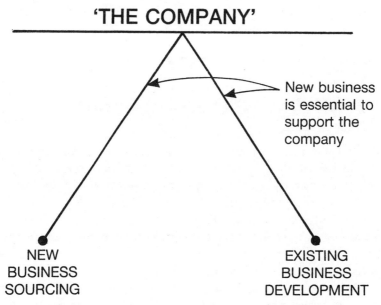

Figure 1 The two aspects of new business getting that support company growth. Each requires a separate technique, and both are different skills to the normal running of the business itself.

And further advice from Rupert?

> Cold calling – on the phone – is yet another skill. Not everyone is good at it, and only a handful of people are brilliant. They

can get the prospects' secretary on their side, for one. [See Chapter 9]

But it's a numbers game in the end. The more calls you make, the more conversions you'll get – either credentials pitches, or the real thing when business is up for grabs.

What system do you need to do that well?

'You need a brought-forward file system to keep accurate records, charm – and one helluva lot of tenacity', concludes Rupert, who estimates that in two years in Young and Rubicam he made 240 pitches – over two per week.

■■■■■■■■■■■■■ **FT Number 9** ■■■■■■■■■■■■■

Remember that new business development requires a different set of skills to those of running a specific business. And recognise the two separate processes of winning new business and developing your existing customer base. Finally, accept that new business requires little magic: it's a numbers game – the more contacts you make, the more you are likely to win.

■■

DO CONFLICTS MATTER?

Before moving on, let me pose a question. Do conflicting interests *really* matter? Or put another way, does it matter if you work for several clients or customers who are in competition with one another – or at least operate within the same industry?

I'll tell you the answer: yes and no. ('No', it doesn't matter to you, but often 'yes' it does matter to a client, you old cynics out there might say.)

But let me give you an example of how it needn't matter a jot. We at QBO had a law firm present to us recently. It was a wondrous occasion; as warming to the cockles as the first time your demented bank manager twigs that you're a sizeable business worth money to his branch – and takes you to lunch. A law firm wanting our business? I yelped when the idea was mooted, conjuring up the prospect of dandruff-ridden gents wiping cobwebs from their faces.

Nothing could have been further from the truth, of course. They were young. They wore double-breasted suits like ad men. They sported loud ties, like PR people do – and came equipped with slides, overhead acetates and a beautifully designed information pack.

But they had more than style – important though that was, and is. They had experience in our sector. They presented therefore, not just how professional indemnity, contractual law and so forth affect *any* business; they told us how they would affect *us*, by giving examples (names not mentioned) of what they'd achieved for others in our world. In short, they specialised in the marketing services sector, and were making a benefit of it.

Does this matter? I wanted to test them, to find out it they had rehearsed a plausible riposte to criticism. So I said:

> This makes me nervous. If you are working for our competitors, how can we be sure our confidential information isn't inadvertently leaked to others?

It was like a red rag to a bull, or could have been. But they countered well, by turning my comment on its head:

> By working in your sector we have amassed vital experience in the special circumstances that surround your business. This can save you money as we can get straight to the nub of the problem, without a learning curve. We can bring experience gained elsewhere in your industry – confidentially – for your benefit.

And so on. It was a good performance. And they embellished it by pointing out that their experience was not just with PR firms like ours, but with sales promotion, direct marketing and advertising firms – so they could bring a whole marketing sector overview to bear.

Now I have to point out that I was mighty pleased with that pitch – because we had coached them. Our training unit at QBO – led by director Francis Hallawell – had taken them on our pitch course and they had boldly decided to try Trevor Morris, QBO's MD and me as their first real-life test.

And they were pretty cute, of course. They knew they were likely to get business from us as a result – who could be so churlish as not to reciprocate? – even if it was in addition to the three other law firms (small, medium and large) that we regularly use at QBO, depending upon the need.

But back to the point. The question is: should you restrict your attempts at new business solely to those prospects that do not conflict with your existing clients or customers?

No, is the answer. Or, not initially, anyhow. You can choose between two options. So, let's clarify the options open to you in structuring your plan.

■■■■■■■■■■■■ **FT Number 10** ■■■■■■■■■■■■

Choose between these two options: offering your services to prospects that are compatible but who do not compete with your existing business, or making a positive benefit out of your industry specialisations. If you decide on the latter option, then segment your specialisms into vertical divisions (eg retail) with its own letterhead mention, mini brochure, etc. If you adopt the former, present your company's horizontal expertise as a whole in terms of its corporate style, philosophy etc in approaching all customer tasks, regardless of industry sector. (See Figure 2.)

■■

OPTION ONE

VERTICAL SECTOR-LED SPECIALISATION

Each division with its own brochure/letterhead within the firm's structure

Each treated as a division within the company

Industry sector

| DRINKS INDUSTRY | RETAIL TRADES | TRAVEL INDUSTRY |

Figure 2a Example of how a law firm or advertising agency might structure its specialist interest in certain market sectors.

OPTION TWO

HORIZONTAL PHILOSOPHY-LED STRUCTURE

Market sectors

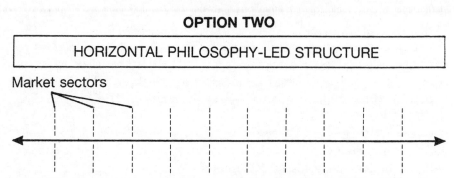

Figure 2b Philosophy-led approach claims principles are portable and that your skills can benefit all clients in all types of industry sector.

So, in summary, there are two further types of ways of picking up business, making three all together:

1. The non-conflict approach using my $(2 + 3) - 1$ formula.
2. A pitch to a client of your competitors *because they approached you* and were then unaware (because they didn't think to ask you) of any conflict. (And why deny them at least a first meeting?)
3. The unsolicited approach to a customer *by you*, knowing that they were already supplied or serviced by one of your competitors.

Notwithstanding the ethical issues surrounding points 2 and 3, which are up to you, the key to prising open a prospect's door to thus open up a dialogue is in all cases by arrangement with a devilish ploy encapsulated in one magic word. That word? 'Credentials'.

And that's what we'll look at in Chapter 3.

WHAT HAVE WE LEARNT?

- How fame matters if you want to be on the shopping list.
- How to formulate a proactive action plan to initially identify new business targets that are non-competitive with your existing business.
- How to hire a graduate trainee to build up a database of information on these targets.
- How to use your prospect's trade press – or industry association handbook – as a cheap source of potential leads and information on their industry. (You can hire someone with specific market experience too, but this will cost more.)
- How to get on with the Wavelength by building a new business culture that permeates throughout the organisation – up and down.
- How to choose between structuring your new business effort into vertical specialisms, or a horizontal company 'philosophy'-led approach.
- How to recognise that getting new business is a different skill to running real existing businesses.

HOW TO PRISE OPEN A PROSPECT'S OFFICE WITHOUT A DOOR WRENCH

3

In which we learn:

- How a 'creds pres' can prise open a closed client door, and how to structure such a 'creds' in real life.
- How to write a successful new business letter.
- How to be modest and non-threatening in attracting Fabbards, Blackguards and Laggards.
- Why a new business prospect is entitled to see you as part of his job spec.
- Why when rolling the new business wheel it needs all the support it can get.
- Why lack of attention to detail is fatal.
- How to successfully use the phone.
- Why it can pay to research the boss as well as the target company.
- How to use the 'correcting technique' to get a prospect's full name.

The credentials pitch is a wonderful little gadget. Correctly positioned, it allows a company to prise open the closed door of its potential client in a way that doesn't threaten anyone – on the face of it, at least. After all, the pitchee (company being pitched to) can justify seeing the pitcher (company pitching) on the basis that he or she, is 'surveying the market-place'.

Imagine the following explanation:

'It's company policy for us to look around occasionally to see what's available from other suppliers'.

That is what a client will say to his ashen-faced supplier when telling him that he has accepted an invitation from that supplier's fiercest competitor for a credentials pitch.

How can the incumbent object or complain? To do so would not just appear defensive, but would actively demonstrate to the beloved client an actual fear of the competitor, which wouldn't say much for the supplier's self-confidence.

Make no mistake, to show even the slightest chink in the armour of supreme confidence (that you are the best supplier that client can get in the entire universe) is one of a business's biggest sins.

Put another way, if you appear to lack that magic ingredient – confidence – then your client will ultimately get the jitters too and the whole relationship will go down the lavatory into the sewers of oblivion.

So next time your biggest customer tells you he's looking around at other suppliers, keep cool. Don't be rattled. Welcome it. Be nonchalant, as if you're not concerned. Why should you be? You'll win out in the end, after all – won't you?

Consider the continuing dialogue:

'But don't be alarmed, Brian,' the client will purr down the phone

It's only a formality – just to see what's also available out there
in your market. We have to look from time to time, you know.
You've done a good job for us, so I can't see much likelihood
of us changing suppliers in the foreseeable future.

'In the foreseeable future . . .'. Classic creepy words, which of course put the fear of God into Brian; classic words, made worse by their jovial rendering from an ever-so-slightly-patronising client, who's secretly enjoying every moment as he imagines Brian's knees knocking and teeth chattering beneath the professional bravado.

But Brian's fear is, of course, your glee: you, the crafty cookie that instigated the credentials invitation with this client in the first place. How did you make it work so effectively (or damagingly, in Brian's case)?

Here's how. You wrote a letter. That simple? Yes.

HOW TO WRITE A SUCCESSFUL LETTER

For years at QBO we've been winging off the same sort of letter, changed only slightly, offering 'creds pres's' to hundreds of firms. And on average probably a third to a half have responded. Which doesn't mean we've got to see all of them, but it's a strike record I'm comfortable with. Here are the key elements to the letter. It should be:

- *modest*: understated, soft sell, succinct;
- *highest status*: personally from Chairman, on his special paper;
- *practical/helpful*: offering case histories, how they can benefit by what you've achieved for others;

- *flattering*: accent on them, not just you;
- *unthreatening*: 'Just to update you on current thinking';
- *call to action*: 'Over a working lunch in our directors' board room so as to bite only into smoked salmon and not to bite too much into your day.'

An example of one of my letters is given below. Looks nothing special at first glance? Dead right – that's the aim. No gimmicks. No verbose Reader's Digest style to deflect the busy prospect for long. No detailed sell made up of a thousand words to plough through. Just a succinct proposition.

Your job – the aim of the letter – is to prise the prospect from behind her desk and plonk her in your conference room for lunch. So you want to create an expectation that she will be informed (and hopefully entertained), in a non-threatening manner.

Not that you plan to wield a club about her person – we know that – but she may feel that she'll be entering the lion's den of the hard sell, never to return alive without one of your invoices and a contract stuffed into her pocket. Your approach should dispel a fear.

Here's the letter: it clearly is about the PR business, but the principle will travel:

Dear Ms Bigbudget,

IS YOUR MARKETING COMMUNICATIONS PROGRAMME
AS EFFECTIVE AS IT COULD BE?

I am writing to personally invite you to a credentials presentation over a working lunch.

The aim will be to demonstrate to you how strategic media relations campaigns can help increase your brand 'share of mind' over your competitors; and to help you build market share.

I would also like to demonstrate to you how our new computerised media relations evaluation system can – like advertising – clearly show to what extent a PR campaign has reached its stated targets, in terms of socio-economic groupings, demographics and to what extent the quality of your messages have been communicated.

We can achieve this by demonstrating our successes for major blue chip clients.

I do hope you are able to accept this invitation: at the very least it will help you to appraise some of the latest developments in the PR business.

We could achieve all we need over lunch in our board room between 12 and 2pm, so as not to bite too much into your time.

Now then, I don't claim to be an expert on direct mail, but all I can say – as witnessed by my increasing waistline – is that it can work.

Not everyone will respond, of course, but that's more a reflection on them than you: most enlightened firms adopt a policy of 'looking around', even if they stay put with their existing supplier in the end.

And referring back to Chapter 2; if you're 'famous' in your field, it's likely the letter will have double the impact – even more so with the added authority of the Chairman.

Not everyone will convert into a customer. But you 'got in through that door', didn't you, without wrenching it open with your jemmy? (Or, at least, you convinced them to walk through your door if they came to visit your office for the lunch.)

HOW TO STRUCTURE A CREDS PRES

The traditional structure I've followed over the years is quite sequential, and can be summed up by adherence to the following sequence of events:

1. history/size/structure;
2. philosophy and people;
3. client list;
4. case histories/special 'issue'.

Taking them one by one, and probably using 35 mm slides, because your investment can be amortised by using the same or a similarly structured creds pres over and over again:

HISTORY/SIZE/STRUCTURE

This will be a rundown on when your firm was founded (and by whom), and how it's grown over the years to its present size (with bar charts if appropriate). It'll also show you teams in action. For example, it may be that you show a colour slide of the planning and research department drawing office, and so forth.

The idea here will not be just to show office areas in isolation, but to demonstrate that you have the systems and structure to solve client problems just like theirs.

Additionally, a photograph on slide of the outside of your office can paint a picture and show the scope of your operations; if you share a first-floor flat in Stockwell, on the other hand, this may be a disadvantage.

PHILOSOPHY AND PEOPLE

This is an important area – if not the most vital – because it can set you totally apart from your competitors: your people and your philosophy are likely to be the most secure discriminators, and the ones unique to you.

If possible you should endeavour to forge your own philosophy – in other words, your own way of doing things, that can again separate you from the crowd, even if in reality you're 'packaging' a standard industry format, but making it your very own.

Equally, show your people – but only if it's relevant. But don't necessarily go through details of the Chairman's history, including snaps of his wife and kids aboard his yacht . . . .

CLIENT LIST

The aim here will be to demonstrate how major or other important organisations now or in the past have entrusted their business to you. The inference is, of course, that if these blue-chip companies have been customers, then why not your Mr Prospect? The best method is to show the logos of these firms or a pack-shot, maybe of their products, if relevant.

CASE HISTORIES/SPECIAL 'ISSUE'

This will be the major thrust of your presentation – the purpose of the pitch. How do you demonstrate that? Firstly, if you use case histories you will do so only if there is a relevance to your audience – nothing is as boring to a client as a pitch about you that bears no relation to his own situation. It'll simply come across as big-headedness on your part – as is described in the next chapter on 'How to think "you", not "me"'.

In my experience, it is nearly always possible to highlight or 'twist' a certain part (or parts) of a case history to make it apposite, especially if you use the flexibility of slides, or an overhead projector (see Top Tips for the Pitch). But the most important aspect of all should be the special 'issue'.

If you refer back to my letter on page 38, the two key issues I raised in my particular case were:

- How we could *demonstrate* that media relations campaigns can help increase brand share of mind and build market share.
- How our new computerised evaluation system could show how a PR campaign has reached its stated targets, just like advertising does.

If the letter had been addressed to an advertising, marketing or communications director in industry, these issues would be most likely to have aroused interest. Don't you think you could devise some similar 'issues' in your own business that could become the psychological link between you and your potential prospect? (see Figure 3).

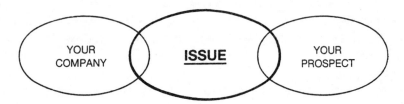

Figure 3 Developing an issue that you know will interest your prospective client will provide a bond between you that could lead to a new business dialogue. It will probably be about an issue which concerns his/her industry or organisation – but definitely not about you.

I'm sure you can.

So you've mounted your creds and started a discussion. And, on the reasonable assumption you didn't screw it up on the day, you should now view that discussion not as an end, but as a beginning of an ongoing dialogue.

■■■■■■■■■■■■ **FT Number 11** ■■■■■■■■■■■■

Most new business isn't always gained immediately. It takes time and effort to build up relationships that can pay off even years later. The fact that a prospect doesn't have a current need, doesn't mean that he won't next year. So keep up a consistent dialogue (without getting on his wick), so that you're remembered when it matters.
■■■

We once pitched to a major company (let's call it Company X), a household name, but we didn't win the business. Not that we were surprised. True, they were on the look-out for a PR firm – so there was a real need – but it quickly transpired after only a few minutes of our credentials that we wouldn't fit the bill. They wanted an investor relations specialist and hadn't make this clear at the outset. It wasn't our bag.

Nevertheless, we had established a contact with two marketing executives who had attended the meeting with the corporate relations man – and that paid handsome dividends over two years later. How come? We literally received a phone call out of the blue to give us some really good news. There was a new chief executive now and he wasn't a man from their industry, but a specialist in marketing. And he had rung the changes.

No longer was Company X going to be product-led, but marketing-led. And, as a result, the two marketing executives, who had liked what they had seen at QBO two years back but had been unable to do anything about it at that time, were now empowered to do so. They had a proper marketing budget and the authority to spend it – on a PR agency.

I don't need to finish the story, do I? But the moral is very meaningful indeed: new business prospects can take years to mature, and some – like this one – come from the most unexpected and obscure directions. So – be consistent in keeping up a dialogue with those already started, no matter how 'dead' they may seem at the time.

THE NEW BUSINESS WHEEL

And so now I can pause to introduce you to the New Business Wheel (see Figure 4).

If you understand the meaning behind the wheel right at the outset, you'll be rolling along the right route towards 'success city'. Here are the four elements of the wheel:

1. *The rim of the wheel* of your new business machine represents your all-pervading corporate reputation (and that of some of your executives who are high profile in your industry).
2. *The downward spoke* represents the new business culture of those on the 'Wavelength' (previously described) that must permeate downwards throughout an organisation from top to bottom – and not just reside in the business development department (or at your graduate trainees department).
3. *The horizontal spoke* in the wheel represents the need for you to continue a consistent dialogue with the new business leads you've already started: if the fish doesn't bite today – and most won't – you can hook him tomorrow – or in two years, as in my example.
4. *The cross-spoke*. This represents cross-selling skills – developing existing business. It's a tremendous opportunity, often overlooked. If you have a client being serviced by you on one aspect of your business, why shouldn't they be tempted to take other services? Well, they won't if you don't have the mechanisms to ask them, that's for sure.

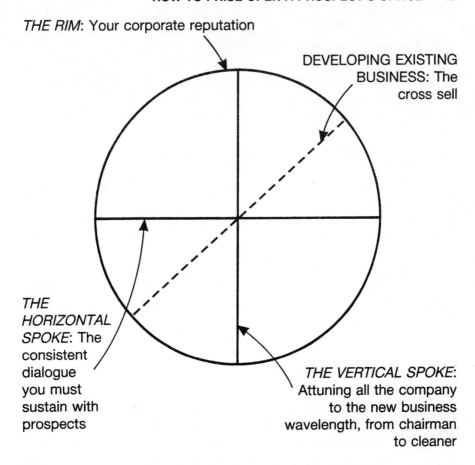

Figure 4 The new business wheel: each spoke supports the rim in order to provide a cohesive business effort that will work effectively.

■■■■■■■■■■■■ **FT Number 12** ■■■■■■■■■■■■

Without these four elements supporting each other in your new business wheel – reputation (rim), internal awareness (downward spoke), continuity of prospect dialogue (horizontal spoke) and developing existing business (cross-spoke) – the complete structure will collapse. In my view, it's as simple as that.
■■

THE NEED FOR PRECISION

Ongoing dialogues with prospects have to be precise. You can't let detail slip, or the effect will be negative. Let me give you an example.

An American PR firm made contact with us at QBO once. Their aim, they said, was to meet several London cousins in their business, in order to build up an informal network. They were on a mission to increase their business by keeping up regular contact with others . . . to create an ongoing dialogue. I admired their proactivity and we dutifully met to exchange creds presentations whilst they were in London.

They were charming people. But a few weeks later we received a thank you letter. It was incorrectly addressed – not even to me – even though they'd met me and talked to me in person for an hour. I felt let down, because they'd created an expectation of professionalism and 'likeability' at the meeting. And then spoiled it.

A few weeks passed, and then I received a mailing with a gimmick – an egg-timer – that basically gave out the message: 'don't waste time – we can help your clients succeed in the USA'.

The inference was that we should use this firm to refer business when we had a need to do so in the USA. I threw it in the bin. Why? It was too clever by half – and impersonal.

First, I figured, they didn't remember my name, and now they are sending mailings which have presumably been dispatched to 100 other PR firms in Europe too.

Finally, I received a personal letter, correctly addressed, asking if I'd like to pitch for one of their US clients who had a need in Europe. They asked for specific experience in the automotive area. Not so bad – it was a specific need – so I felt loved again.

I faxed back, saying we had previously had such experience, but that our entire philosophy – as I'd explained before to them in person and in great detail – presented QBO as a firm whose skill was to plan 'PR Solutions to Marketing Problems'. Our skill was horizontal – providing PR solutions regardless of industry specialisation, and a successfully proven skill, at that. But we'd be pleased to pitch on that basis as we normally do.

Can you guess what happened? I had no reply, except that is, yet another bland, impersonal mailing . . . . The moral? It is so important it deserves an FT.

■■■■■■■■■■■■ **FT Number 13** ■■■■■■■■■■■■

If you start a new business dialogue, you must pay excruciating and assiduous attention to detail to ensure that all contact is personal, personalised and above all, co-ordinated and consistent (and I believe without gimmicks, too).
■■

Let me give you another real life example. I welcome it when I get a good letter from someone wanting to sell me something. I don't call it junk mail. I like it. I'm happy to be given the opportunity of deciding whether I bin something, or take action. I like having the choice.

But I hate it, as happened recently, when it falls flat because of a lack of follow up – because of lack of attention to detail and co-ordination. In this case, I had responded to an excellent letter from a well-known computer supplier, as I was looking for a laptop.

What could have been better? I was in the market and they had pitched to me in a way I liked. So I responded to their offer for more details – to the marketing manager personally, as suggested in his own letter to me. Then it all collapsed. No 'delivery of the promise'.

'What offer's that, sir?', asked the girl enquiringly when I telephoned, as instructed by their letter and leaflet:

> Oh, is there another offer? We get many like that. Just hold, I'll have to check . . . . The marketing manager? Oh, I'm afraid he's not here today. Well, actually he's too busy normally to take these calls himself (nervous giggle).

As it happened, I bought their laptop, but it was purely because of the product itself and the financial deal I screwed out of them as a result of the computer recession.

But maybe I should have told them to stuff it where no one likes to go. Why? Because they insulted me, disappointed me. They created an expectation of personal contact – like the US PR firm – and then treated me like a commodity. So beware! Be personal. Co-ordinate your mailings so they link. Keep assiduous details on file of your contacts, and their comments last time on the replies received. Match the delivery to the promise.

KNOWING THE INDIVIDUAL

Which brings me to another aspect that paradoxically began in America: getting information on the individual in your target company.

Once you've got your man or woman in for that creds lunch, you'll also get to know a bit about them personally. Do they like golf? Live in Hampshire? Collect antique spoons? Dress up in ladies underwear (the men, I mean)?

Without using torture, or appearing to be too forward, you can prise fascinating information from the individual. And, by carefully detailing their information on your files, you can – subtly – use it again. To feed back to them to demonstrate your genuine interest.

How? Add a handwritten postscript on your next personal letter, for example. Or, at your next meeting, raise it in conversation. It all helps to demonstrate that you and he are not robots, but people. And if you endear prospects to you – besides showing a capability of handling their business, of course – you're likely to hold an advantage over your competitors. But don't overdo it, or you'll be thought rude, intrusive and impertinent. The British value highly their 'space', remember.

But back to the letter you sent to prospects, and the growing list of contacts. How do you manage it as it begins to grow? Well, firstly you can divide and file your ongoing database of such prospects (gleaned from their trade journals and other ways, as previously described) into three categories: those that replied accepting your 'pitch' for credentials – the 'fabbards', because they are fabulous; those that said 'no' – the blackguards; and those that didn't grace you with a reply – the laggards.

You need to file them in different categories – and you don't necessarily need a computer database, although that helps enormously. (An old-fashioned binder file will do.)

Let's take them one-by-one.

THE FABBARDS

The first category is self-evident: you get a date in the diary for the credentials to take place, as described previously in this chapter.

THE BLACKGUARDS

For the second category you adopt a slightly different approach. Why? Because although their response was negative, you've received a hint of interest, as evidenced by the fact that they actually responded.

OK, he or she may have coined the normal sort of bland clichés in so doing. You know the sort of thing:

> We currently are well served by our existing supplier and therefore see no reason to change. But thank you for thinking of the Scunthorpe Screw Co . . . and so on.

Do you stop the dialogue there? No. One major advertising agency is renowned for its policy of not giving up on a prospect simply because they've said no, or even when they have appointed someone else. And they're right – notably because they've notched up considerable success in recapturing business lost, the second time around.

A recent article in *Campaign* magazine ('The death of the pitch is nigh' by John Tylee, 30 October, 1992) stated:

> in part, the increasing ingenuity within [advertising] agencies at keeping the dialogue going with a business prospect, even after a failed pitch, is being fuelled by the high cost of staging a presentation. With up to £30,000 being staked on a contest for a £5 million account, there is a huge reluctance to allow that investment to be wasted.

Well, you may not match up to those million pound figures, but the principle still applies to you. You put time and effort into it, didn't you? And time is money, isn't it?

THE LAGGARDS

You take this lot as a challenge. And you like challenges, don't you? Remember one thing – just because you haven't received a reply doesn't necessarily mean there is no interest in your proposition. Your letter may have been put aside for future action. Or put in a pending file, stuck in a briefcase – and so on. So there's no need necessarily to take offence, or get the hump. Instead, give these laggards the benefit of the doubt: assume that, at the very worst, they've mislaid your missive rather than binned it. So, in short, keep up the dialogue.

But how? Repeat your offer, or one like it – and do this three or four times a year. But no more. Always refer to the date of your last letter in a new one, to show continuity – and to hopefully engender a tiny bit of guilt in your uncooperative target.

Always check, incidentally (or get your graduate trainee to check) if the key guy or woman is still the key person – by phoning their switchboard. Say: 'I'm writing to your finance director, Mr Shilling – can I check his spelling and initials?' They'll soon tell you if he's left – and who's taken over, for you to change your records and act accordingly.

■■■■■■■■■■■■ **FT Number 14** ■■■■■■■■■■■■

A company switchboard operator can be a mine of information, if handled properly, in terms of giving the names and functions of your potential prospects.
■■

Our ruse is to link into what I call the 'correcting technique'.

The correcting technique

Let's imagine you need to know the name of the marketing director of a company. If you ring up and ask outright, it's possible that the operator may be suspicious of such an enquiry, and thus become reluctant to impart the information. She'll most likely believe you are selling something (she'd be right!) and feel it her duty to defend her boss from the likes of you. But the information will just flow from her lips if you use the 'correcting technique'. How?

Just say to her on the phone: 'I'm writing to your marketing director today; it *is* Mr Graham Smith, isn't it?' 'Oh no' she'll retort our marketing director is Ms Sheila Jones.'

See the point? She'll have abandoned any defensive mode in order to correct you. It's human nature. What a wheeze!

USING THE PHONE

But there are other more effective ways of using the phone. Whether we are dealing with Laggard, Blackguard or Fabbard, the blower is a major new business weapon we have thus far not highlighted.

Cold-calling a prospect on the telephone is in theory an excellent wheeze. But I dislike it, and feel that it can be fraught with danger. Why? Because I'm convinced that inherent in the British character is a distaste for the good old blower. Unlike many Europeans, and certainly the Americans, we suffer from 'phone phobia'. Callers 'bug' us by disturbing our peace. Nowhere is this more true than when it comes to being hassled by a high-powered sales pitch, and I caution you against mounting such a campaign. Such highly-trained people – selling anything from insurance to advertising space – can easily get up the victim's nose.

It invades their space, puts their backs up. And what way to sell is that? I should know: as a youngster I went through the renowned Thomson newspaper tele-ad training course, before being let loose to flog classified advertising space down the phone line.

It didn't last long. Not that I was fairly useless, only totally useless. It was because I was sensitive to the hackles as I felt them begin to rise on my victim on the other end of the line. I could sense the metaphorical drawbridge being raised in the brain of my unfortunate prospect, as I went through my blurb.

It was then I realised that trying to push water uphill was not the most clever way of selling.

▪▪▪▪▪▪▪▪▪▪▪▪ **FT Number 15** ▪▪▪▪▪▪▪▪▪▪▪▪

The best way to sell is to make a prospect buy – it's a subtle but true difference worth learning. Hassling on the telephone at a time convenient to you but not to your prospect flies in the face of this advice.
▪▪

Like all generalisations, however, this is only partly true, of course. There are excellent telephone sales people. And there are gullible or soft prospects that agree to anything for a quiet life.

However, a recent article in *Design Week* – an industry publication – tackled the thorny question of sales pitches on the phone as undertaken by design firms in the search for new business.

It didn't paint it in a very good light. According to the article, one client summed up the feelings of others by saying he hated

> persistent sales people who assume my secretary is education-ally sub-normal and insist on speaking to me – only to get the same response my secretary would have given them.

(See also the section on 'getting the secretary on your side', in Chapter 9.)

Another client was quoted as saying: 'blabbering on about their company without asking if I've got time to listen annoys me, because it's discourteous.'

Yet another spluttered:

> telephone calls are the most annoying. Some people are very difficult to get off the phone and there's no way any of these are going to get to present to us.

And the answer? In my view, the trick is not to cold-call on the phone simply to offer a meeting. It is better to use the phone to *follow up* an invitation of some sort that strikes a positive note in your prospect, not a negative one.

It is all to do with taking that 180 degree shift from trying to sell *me*, into offering something specific for *you*. And that's what we'll examine next in Chapter 4: that change of emphasis from *me* to *you*, because this new attitude to life is vital if you want your prospects' budgets – even from those who were billed as Blackguards and Laggards – to leap from their bank accounts into yours.

WHAT HAVE WE LEARNT?

■ A credentials letter can get you through the door by appealing to a prospect's sense of fair play and even duty in 'surveying the market-place'.

■ The vital importance of recognising the reputation, awareness and consistency that make up a new business wheel, and how each support the other.

■ How to structure a pitch from history/size/structure, through to that special 'issue'.

■ The importance of paying assiduous attention to precision, by keeping detailed records.

■ The importance of paying attention to the person, as well as the company.

■ How keeping up a dialogue is the best way to deal with even the blackguards and laggards.

■ How to be wary of using the phone in a 'cold-call' situation.

4 HOW TO THINK 'YOU' NOT 'ME'

GETTING THE RIGHT FRAME OF MIND TO PITCH

In which we learn:

- How to get prospects to buy your service, without overtly asking them.
- The psychology of engendering the right positive response from prospects – even the 'blackguard' and 'laggard' varieties.
- How to tempt prospects into attending your seminar or meeting by talking to them . . . about themselves.
- Why there's a taxi driver in all of us.
- How you can win the pitch in the 'interlude', months before you even do it.
- How to use research, and the 'concept' to pull in new clients.
- Why 'you' new business vehicles are limited only by your own energy and imagination.

I want now to touch on a delicate point: how vital it is to overcome your inherent love of yourself, and instead slant the pitch away from just your own attributes – however charming these may be – towards those of your prospect.

This throws into perspective the one weakness of the credentials type of pitch: by definition, it leans towards *me*.

It has to, of course.

'How else can I inform potential business prospects about *my* successes, philosophy and points of difference over *my* competitors without a degree of self-indulgence?', you rightly ask. (And we all love a bit of that.)

Scores of ad agencies and PR firms are hired each year on the strengths of their myopic and mostly insular 'showreel' – or corporate video – which is available for prospects to view in private at an organisation called the Advertising Agency Register (and its sister, the

PR Register). And many business relationships – perhaps worth millions of pounds sterling – are born that way.

So credentials presentations can – and do – work well in terms of exciting a prospect enough to want to risk an ongoing relationship with you; and what's more, to part with money, which has got to be your prime objective, after all.

But let's just linger on the creds a little longer. The very best come from those exponents who are clever enough to be able to make a prospect feel that the case histories you show of work for others are – or could be – relevant to him. It's a great skill.

Two different experts can make the same type of credentials presentation, but with different results. One will make it seem that he is saying: 'Look how brilliant we are.'

The other, better expert, will demonstrate how this technique, successfully proven for another client, can be successfully adapted to suit the client's needs.

Think about it. So many companies can tend to get hooked on self-congratulatory presentations of credentials, preening themselves as they talk about the thing most dear to them: themselves, and how clever they are. It can easily happen, and I should know, it's happened to me. Has it to you?

Next time you give a credentials presentation, practice delivering it from the potential client perspective, and see how much better it works.

But I have some good news. There are even better methods to try and hook new prospects that – unlike the creds – place the emphasis firmly on the *you*, rather than the *me*. And as such they stand more chance of hooking in our recently described Blackguard (who said no) and Laggard (who didn't say anything).

They teach us a tremendously important lesson: how getting acquainted with our potential client (or client industry) *before our pitch* is often the key to winning it.

How? By glancing away from ourselves and looking – well before the pitch – into the camp of our prospects. It's a 180 degree change of direction, a fundamental change of emphasis which, when learnt, can pay great dividends. There are mechanisms to help us crystalise this change of emphasis, and I'll describe them shortly.

THEIR WINNING WAYS: PETER GUMMER

But first let me quote from Peter Gummer, Chairman of Shandwick plc, one of the world's largest PR firms, who told me over lunch one day, when we were discussing life in general and this book:

The period preparing for the pitch, where one goes through the process of getting to know the client intimately and to identify his problem, is by far the most important aspect. So important is it, that undertaken expertly, it can build a relationship or partnership in the early days that actually on occasions renders a formal pitch unnecessary.

Peter is a wise man: look at Figure 5 below to see how my pitch triangle sums up what he was alluding to. Is he talking about an extreme circumstance? Or is this where the future lies? You can make up your own mind, but if, by taking his advice, we can win a pitch in that month or two of interlude before we actually make the presentation, then that's got to be the best thing since your first sexual climax, hasn't it? (Or was that your second climax?)

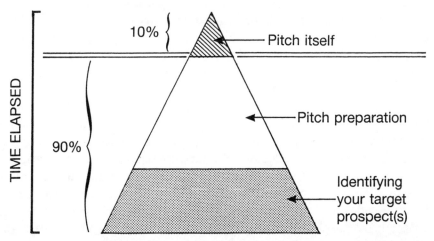

Figure 5 The majority of time and preparation is spent below-the-line. In a successful organisation, only 10 per cent of the activity represents the pitch itself.

In a *Campaign* magazine article, Sue Farr, corporate communications director of Thames TV was quoted as saying, 'It's at that time that your impressions of an agency are reinforced or blown out of the water.' She was, of course, referring to what I've described as the 'interlude' between an agency being selected for a pitch, and the pitch itself.

During that time agencies will naturally want to get as close to their prospect as possible – and to get as much background information as possible in order to achieve an edge over their similarly eager competitors.

For some this opportunity may indeed be an advantage. For others, it might 'blow them out of the water'. Additionally, one ad agency director said in the same article that 'It's much more competitive in the pre-pitch period, because agencies know they have to get in at a very early stage.'

And that, of course, means it's much better to have established contacts with potential prospects, through a policy of continuous dialogue so you're in that frame when the opportune time comes.

'The showbiz and dazzle of a setpiece pitch is still irresistible for a lot of clients,' another adman says in the *Campaign* feature, 'but those who prefer to work by building relationships [early on] are growing in number.'

But back to the *you* over the *me*. We all love the sound of our own voice – some more than others. And yet, most of us simply do not recognise that our pitchee doesn't care a jot about our voice, or the sound of it. He cares about himself and his or her voice first and foremost.

Let's just think of the psychology of this for a second. Imagine yourself in a taxi. Now, I have nothing against cabbies, and most of them are charming people who acquit their duties behind the wheel in our increasing traffic jams, with grace and efficiency. (Well, efficiency, anyway.) But we've all met The Bore, haven't we? He's the cabbie that, because he's had yet another frustrating day, is eager to tell you all about it. You know, the bad driving, the road works, the jams, etc.

But he's forgotten something, hasn't he? He's forgotten that you're not interested. Because you too have had a busy day, and all you want to do is relax in the tranquility of a silent cab until you reach your destination: another meeting. You want to mentally plan it, but you can't.

And still the cabbie drones on. And on. About the road conditions. About why 'they' dig the road up here, or 'they' make a one-way system there. (Who are 'they' anyway?) Now you can't blame him necessarily because his life centres around those problems. But yours doesn't. And that's the point I'm making. You don't care about his tactical problems *en route* – you have simply paid him to get there. The cabbie assumes, because the problems he faces are real to him, that they will be real to you as well. He's thinking only of *me* and not at all about *you*. And so it is with the psychology of pitching.

■■■■■■■■■■■■ **FT Number 16** ■■■■■■■■■■■■

To get a positive response – which is what you want – think about how the receiver of your messages will assess what you say, because it must be driven by his needs, wants, fears, pride, aspirations, and a host of his other emotions.

■■■

Don't get carried away talking about yourself just because you are (albeit rightly) proud of your work. In short, don't fall into the trap of assuming that because Mr Prospect has asked you to tell him about yourself or your firm, he actually wants to know.

Do mention yourself, of course. But don't do it to the exclusion of your prospect (the receiver of your messages), because otherwise your effectiveness will be like that of a sports car's powerful engine, without the necessary gearbox to transmit the power on to the road. And what good is that? None.

And remember the key words in the FT above: receiver and response. As the pitcher, you are the transmitter, but you're only an effective one if you create the right response to your message. And to do that, talk in terms of *you*, not *me*.

So what *you* methods can we use to attract new business? I'm going to give you several sequential examples. They are:

■ the market survey;
■ the seminar;
■ the leaflet;
■ the interview.

Let's take them one by one.

THE MARKET SURVEY ON YOUR PROSPECT'S MARKET

What can a market survey achieve apart from drain money from your own bank account to research people? I'll tell you. It can provide market data on a target industry that a company operating in that industry would find hard – if not impossible – to ignore.

Let's take three examples of professional services firms endeavouring to target advertising agencies as new business prospects.

THE LAW FIRM

You might take the following issues as your subject:

Professional indemnity

You might want to chart the perceptions that advertising agencies (your identified target market) hold regarding the latest developments in professional indemnity. Are they fully conversant, or blissfully unaware?

Contracts

Are they watertight? Are advertising agencies keeping abreast of all the new loopholes?

THE ACCOUNTANCY PRACTICE

Alternatively, let's imagine you are an accountancy practice. There are possible subjects amongst ad agencies as your target group, such as:

Cash flow forecasts

Are they completed properly? Are ad people too bound up in their creative environment to worry about how good cash flow equates with profit?

Computerised timesheets

Are agencies using all the state of the art technology to determine their profitable charge-out times? If not, are they losing money?

These are just two simplistic examples to illustrate my point, of course. But the same principle applies to all issues in all industries: what you are doing in this case is to ask a sample of ad agencies how they feel about certain key issues that affect them, and about which you too have more than a casual interest. Why?

First, because everyone enjoys being asked their opinion about the things they have an opinion on concerning their livelihood.

And second, because the results of such an exercise will, you can bet, provide you with – if not surprises – then a number of 'pegs' to feed back to them and on which to hang other new business techniques like, for example, a small seminar programme, based around the findings of your survey. Let me give you a hypothetical example.

THE SEMINAR

Let's say – as a law firm – you discover that the majority of ad agencies surveyed by you don't realise their vulnerability in the market-place when it comes to professional indemnity. Certain recent precedents have been set in the Courts. Agencies can now be sued for vast sums of money as principals if the advertisements they produce don't meet certain standards.

Or, your survey could have revealed that a worrying majority of agencies are at risk of losing considerable sums of money simply because their contracts are not watertight in relation to current legal thinking.

Now, these are entirely hypothetical and simplistic examples to make a point. I am not necessarily condoning the use of shock tactics. But you will agree that an invitation to agency financial directors or chief executives inviting them to a seminar (or even a simple meeting – you don't need a seminar) at which this and other topics that are of direct concern to them are discussed, has a better chance of getting them to meet you than a straight 'we want to work for you' type of approach, wouldn't you? (Well, you should.) Why? Because:

■ You've hooked their interest in themselves.
■ You've talked about *you*, not about *me*.
■ You're going to offer them a solution to the potential problem you raised.

And it's that last part, of course, that coincides with your own commercial interest – and there's absolutely nothing wrong with that.

So, if it transpires that awareness of their vulnerability to being sued by clients is lamentably low, then you as a law practice have a right to claim a certain skill in assisting agencies to plug the gap in their defences. And, in short, to sell your services.

Equally, if most small agencies from your survey appear not to appreciate that profit without positive cash flowing into your bank is pretty useless, then you – as an accountancy practice – can gently point out ways of getting the outstanding debts inwards. And you can explain in the process how you can add to their bottom-line profitability. Or, in short, sell your services.

There are other types of survey, of course – and some of them can cost the sponsor many thousand of pounds. For example, an advertising agency might commission a market research organisation to establish attitudes amongst different groups of consumers towards Japanese cars.

The results might make fairly riveting reading for the marketing directors of Japanese car firms that market in the UK. And, as such, it's a pretty sure bet that that ad agency will get an audience with a number of manufacturers, even if they have done their own research.

The same *Campaign* article previously mentioned agrees with me:

> Keep the lines of communications open . . . that means getting the prospect [back*] into the agency, perhaps to see a relevant piece of research.

But what happens if you don't have access to any particularly relevant and topical research such as described above? You can still achieve your aims by 'going concept'.

THE CONCEPT MEETING

There is another method of luring prospects into your office (or enticing them to let you into theirs) – one that doesn't necessitate your paying for any original research into a client's business.

This method takes a less-focused view and instead looks more widely at the client's 'world' in general. I call it the Concept – and it serves the similar role of bridging a prospect's interests with your own: a sort of new-business bonding not unlike the one described in Chapter 3 relating to the creds presentation letter – but more in-depth this time.

Let me give you an example. Towards the end of 1992 I developed a new-business presentation called 'The World is Changing'. What I did was to put on to slide some general thoughts my colleagues and I had had for some time about the changing nature of the marketing services business and how the character and substance of marketing communications were (so we felt) about to alter in relation to a changing world.

So, we charted how the media was changing (eg increase of cable and TV programme sponsorship, and changes in the BBC); how consumers' needs could change (eg the seeking of difference in the products and services they buy – to keep away from the Joneses); how marketing requirements could change (eg less glib and patronising TV advertisements and the creation of more dialogues through below-the-line activities such as direct marketing and PR); and how, finally, clients' needs could alter as a result of all of these points.

So what's so different about the 'Concept'? Simply that it actually reverts back to 'me'. That's because it is our view of the world and as such it is not directly about them, although it will impact on them. It is also speculation, and not 'fact'. But what it does do is to provide that 'bridge of interest' between us and a potential client. It provides food for thought, and by allowing us to enter their world it helps to bond us to the potential client by allowing us to share our mind with his or hers.

What's subtle and interesting about these techniques is that when

* See also Chapter 9, 'After the Pitch'.

you have your new business prospect in front of you, you have no need to ram your services down his or her throat. By simply raising an issue of concern you will have put in train a thought process in your target prospect that may end up with the client popping the question: 'What can you do about this?' Or, 'How do you think we can adapt to these changes that are taking place?'

Let them make the move, on the basis that the best way to sell is to goad people into buying. In short, let them make the decision to hire you – without overtly having asked them. The principle is one I hope you'll grasp with both hands, and your feet to boot.

OK, what is the vital principle we have proved by adopting this technique? Here's what you've proved to your potential client market (ad agencies in this example – but it can apply universally). It is that you understand their business – a part of the arena in which they operate.

Remember that survey I mentioned that revealed that 95 per cent of clients rated 'understanding products or services' (for which read also 'understanding my business market') as the best way for a supplier to get shortlisted? This is a way for you to leap 1,000 hurdles straight to the shortlist – because you don't have to wait ten years to gain experience in a sector.

You have simply demonstrated an understanding today, courtesy of your survey that charted their industry's attitudes, and which revealed their misunderstandings. This allowed you to feed the findings back to them to start a dialogue with key people. And it put you at great risk of winning a piece of new business as a result. Not necessarily now, today. But you're in business for the long haul, after all, aren't you? So, wait for tomorrow.

■■■■■■■■■■■■ **FT Number 17** ■■■■■■■■■■■■

Don't underestimate the power of initial contact itself. Meeting prospects face-to-face and leaving an impression (hopefully favourable) is in itself a major achievement that will, in time, pay dividends. It's like putting money into a deposit account: you will be able to draw on the resources later on.
■■

And you don't have to go to the lengths of a seminar, of course (if you do, you should hire a PR firm to do it for you, in my view):

■ You can have the simple meeting that I mentioned, or mount the smaller-sounding 'workshop', where just two or three guests are present.

- Alternatively, you could arrange to speak on your topic at a major conference organised by a third party, like their trade association, for example. That way they pay the costs, and you may even get a fee. **Big message:** Some of the most effective new business ploys or PR programmes can be self-financing.
- Or you could simply write letters asking for that one-to-one meeting.

But most importantly you can be seen as *the* expert on that issue at the meeting, seminar, workshop or conference – and make mileage from that. How?

THE SPECIALIST LEAFLET

All you need is your firm's own specialist 'vertical' leaflet – charting within it relevant facts and figures from your survey, to which is added the associated services and skills you offer. You can mail this to prospects in that 'vertical' industry – followed up by telephone calls from your by now overworked graduate trainee new-business executive.

THE INTERVIEW

Finally, you can even arrange an interview on your findings with a relevant local radio business programme, if applicable, or more likely undertake a media relations campaign directed at the trade press – depending on the quality and news-worthiness of the material. And it's all on the back of your survey and supporting seminar and leaflet.

■■■■■■■■■■■■ **FT Number 18** ■■■■■■■■■■■■

What you are really doing is employing subtle PR tactics to win new business: 'creating' an issue which raises a valid problem – and which then offers a product or service to help solve that problem – is a key PR role.

■■■

But in addition to just massaging your personal ego and corporate reputation via any media coverage that this could engender, it can also (as in this case) help you begin a new business dialogue with key target prospects. Because with luck your PR coverage will attract phone calls from interested prospects.

So there. Your market survey has provided you with enough data to enable you to package it into various new business vehicles:

- seminar, workshops, or meeting;
- specialist 'vertical'leaflet used as a mailer with letter for a one-to-one meeting to follow.

And to cap it all, you've also made yourself vulnerable to a chat with the trade press, and maybe even an after-dinner speech on the subject. Is there any end to it all, you ask? No, is the answer. These vehicles are limited only by your own energy and imagination.

Having attracted all this interest, how do you manage all the likely resulting pitches? That's what we'll now examine next in detail, starting with the issue of the pitching environment.

WHAT HAVE WE LEARNT?

- To ensure our pitch emphasises the *you*: what the prospect wants and will need, however, rather than the service you offer. That will follow naturally.
- How a market survey can reveal data a target industry will want to know about, and how you can use it to start a dialogue.
- How the survey can form the basis of a meeting, seminar, workshop, etc.
- How the same information can be used as the basis of a PR campaign of media interviews and/or coverage aimed at your prospect's trade press.
- That making face-to-face contact with prospects is an achievement in itself, and is like putting money in a deposit account to draw on later.
- How survey data can be turned into a vertical industry leaflet and used at your seminars as a 'give-away' or as direct mail to other companies in that industry.

HOW TO ASSESS THE PITCH ENVIRONMENT

(AND TO REACT ACCORDINGLY)

In which we learn:

- Why the pitch environment timeframe and the attitude of the audience matter.
- How to use anecdotes as Red Indian signals.
- Why 30 seconds is longer than you think.
- Why radio audiences are semi-captive and new business pitches sweaty.
- The trouble with jokes, and why you can make pertinent points entertainingly, but never serious points flippantly.

Most eminent books on presentations don't appear to deeply consider the effect of 'where' one is pitching. Their preoccupation appears to surround the tactics and techniques of the event itself: how to breathe, pause, overcome objections, etc. All important stuff, of course, but they pale into insignificance once you've got the 'shield of confidence' in front of you, as we'll discuss in Chapter 6.

There's another fundamental issue, often forgotten, that I'd like to highlight first: the pitch environment. But just let me remind you at this point of the other fundamental issues that we've already encountered in previous chapters.

RECAP

1. We've looked at how one identifies non-competitive prospects in the first place.
2. We've examined how one then breaks down their doors, metaphorically speaking, to meet them via a credentials presentation.
3. And we've investigated how, by triggering knowledge and attitude

research into their market-place, we are able to use this as a peg to justify talking to them about *them*, rather than just ourselves, in a process that could start a new business dialogue – not least because you have a service to sell on the coat-tails of the problem, you little scamp.

And we did all this for the simple reason that we discovered that getting a face-to-face dialogue to demonstrate that we understand a prospect's business in the first place – and particularly well before the pitch – has proved to be the single most important aspect. In short, we're helping you up the church aisle, because without that trip how can you expect to marry the bride?

Well, there's another fundamental aspect that's just as important to stress before we move on to the technique of the pitch itself, in my view. It relates to the environment.

Cast your eyes to Figure 6 below and you'll see what I mean. Let's look in this instance beyond the new business pitch and consider how each of the following pitch environments differ:

▪ radio/TV interview;
▪ seminar/conference;
▪ after-dinner speech;
▪ new business pitch.

What is important here is to appreciate just how much each of these different pitch environments will influence the style of approach one adopts.

Let's take them one by one. Each relate to two things: timeframe and audience attitude.

RADIO/TV INTERVIEW

Timeframe

Notwithstanding the fact that they induce a fear that can melt your kneecaps, the most overwhelming aspect about a TV or radio environment is its inherent 'succinctness'. On a radio interview, you'll be very lucky to get three or four minutes of valuable air-time, and sometimes only as little as 10 or 15 seconds: a tiny timeframe in which to get across your key messages.

Of course, some radio interviews can last as long as 45 minutes (especially if you're lucky enough, as I have been, to join chat-type programmes) but I reckon on average you get a miniscule 15 to 30 seconds. You therefore have to adapt accordingly by learning how to compress your key messages down the line.

RADIO/TV INTERVIEW	AFTER DINNER SPEECH	NEW BUSINESS PITCH	SEMINAR/ CONFERENCE
Timeframe	*Timeframe*	*Timeframe*	*Timeframe*
15–30 seconds or 4–8 minutes*	20 minutes optimum	60–90 minutes (with questions)	30–45 minutes
Audience attitude:	*Audience attitude*:	*Audience attitude*:	*Audience attitude*:
■ Semi-captive, casual ■ Little pre-conception	■ Formal, but paradoxically casual as well	■ Formal and structured ■ Captive ■ Pre-conceptions will need living up to . . .	■ Formal ■ Captive ■ Expectant (They paid to hear you!)
Dialogue or monologue?	*Dialogue or monologue?*	*Dialogue or monologue?*	*Dialogue or monologue?*
100% dialogue	95% monologue	60% monologue	75% monologue
All require forethought for potential questions			

* depends upon whether it's a newspiece or a feature item

Figure 6   The differing pitch environments at a glance.

ASIDE

Thirty seconds is actually longer than most people think it is. A lawyer colleague of mine once summed it up well when he described going to a gymnasium for the first time, recently. He was put on the weights to build his biceps. 'When I was told to do it for 30 seconds, I thought it would be a doddle,' he recalls, 'but now the pain reminds me how long 30 seconds really is.' And so it is with interviews, pain or not!

Audience attitude

Radio listeners, unlike most TV addicts, are a mobile bunch. How many of us, I wonder, are doing other things, whilst taking in bits and bobs of a background burble called the radio (or mother-in-law, in my case) as well? Quite a few, I would wager, although this doesn't apply to drive-time between six and nine in the morning and four and seven in the evening, of course. Generally speaking, TV and radio pro-grammes are wallpaper: the audience (your receiver) is thus semi-captive, but casual as well.

What does this mean to the pitcher (or in this case the interviewee)? It means you have got to be succinct and clear with your messages, so that they can penetrate the skulls of your wandering audience, despite the fact that they are negotiating a hairpin bend in their Ferrari; vacuuming the cat at home; or reading *Penthouse* deftly hidden within the *Financial Times* in front of the telly. In short, they are doing other things *as well as* listening to (or looking at) you. (A Top Tip for isolating key messages and sticking to them is discussed in Chapter 7.)

SEMINAR/CONFERENCE

Timeframe

One can be much more expansive in this mode – one hour representing the maximum; twenty minutes to half an hour the norm (for an individual slot, that is).

Can you be more self-indulgent then? No, not self-indulgent exactly, but you can enjoy the relative luxury of expanding your key points into sub-points, and adding mental and visual illustrations that underline your messages. (See also Top Tip Number 1, Chapter 7). This again requires a different technique in relation to the different environment.

Audience attitude

The audience will be more formal here, of course. And *captive*. But more than that, they'll be expectant. Whereas a radio or TV interview may reach listeners or viewers without necessarily any preconceptions, a seminar or conference will create an expectation that needs to be fulfilled. And this may simply be because the audience – the receivers of your message – have actually paid to hear your pearls of wisdom. And if they pay for something, they want – expect – value for money, don't the little dears? I would, for one. So it is essential that, in addition to appreciating the more formal nature of the proceedings, you give the audience what they half expect and another half they do not, besides.

Remember, too, this format can often be as much as a 25 per cent two-way dialogue – just like radio or TV, but not as severe. In other words, you'll get questions based on what you've said – so you must be ready to give the (appropriate and pithy) answer.

And here's an FT that applies to all pitches, regardless of type.

▪▪▪▪▪▪▪▪▪▪▪▪ **FT Number 19** ▪▪▪▪▪▪▪▪▪▪▪▪

You've to prepare, at this point, a questions and answers scenario, to identify and rehearse your answers *in advance* to the likely questions you can expect, in order to hit for six the potential googlies which will be hurled at you.

▪▪

AFTER DINNER SPEECH

Timeframe

Twenty minutes is the optimum here, I believe. Any longer, and the minds of the audience will only be partly with you, with the other part probably enjoying a sunbathe on a sandy beach in Barbados – or wistfully cavorting between the sheets with their new secretary or boss. In their imagination, of course.

But wait: even after four or five minutes their attentiveness will begin to wander, so although again they've often paid for the privilege of hearing and seeing you, they may not extend to you the courtesy of actually *listening*. Not that you'll ever know, of course, apart from the odd yawn, whispering between friends, clinking of glasses or, in the extreme – an ungrateful diner nodding off. So, beware!

▪▪▪▪▪▪▪▪▪▪▪▪ **FT Number 20** ▪▪▪▪▪▪▪▪▪▪▪▪

Remember the simple rule: the longer you drone on, the less effective you are likely to be. Only the most expert speakers can hold an audience riveted for more than twenty minutes.

▪▪

Audience attitude

This is an interesting one, a paradox even. Why? Because although the audience will, on the face of it, be in a formal mode (the black tie and dinner jacket will testify to that) they in fact require a more *casual* approach.

And that's precisely why so many after-dinner speakers fail: they fall between the two stools, being either too flippant, or too serious. The sum result is that they become too boring, or even embarrassing.

■■■■■■■■■■■■ **FT Number 21** ■■■■■■■■■■■■

Make all your pertinent points in an entertaining way, if you can. But never make serious points in a flippant or jokey manner. It's a fine distinction to recognise.

■■

SIGNALS AND ANECDOTES

What does this mean in practice? Simply that if you attempt to turn your key messages into a flippant joke, you will confuse your audience. Are you being serious, or telling a joke? They won't know, because you've been imprecise. You haven't given them the appropriate signals.

That's why I carefully use the word 'pertinent' instead of 'serious'; and 'entertaining' instead of 'jokey'. And the key to achieving the latter? Anecdotes, that's what.

In short: tell a tale to illustrate your point and – yes – you'll probably make people titter as well. But your message will not be obscured – your point will be well made, and will have hit home.

Be flippant, on the other hand, and your audience won't know whether to laugh, or appear to be thoughtful, even serious. And the brain, being confused, will discard what you've said altogether because it's getting conflicting messages. And you'll fail.

But back to environment, and our final segment: the new-business pitch.

THE NEW-BUSINESS PITCH

Timeframe

One hour and a half is the optimum, although two hours is not uncommon (see Q5, Chapter 11). As we'll discuss later, the pitch should be divided into three sections:

■ A 'Why we're suitable' summary.
■ A 'What we recommend for you today'.
■ A question session.

THEIR WINNING WAYS: WINSTON FLETCHER

According to Winston Fletcher, the advertising guru whose name has arguably been bolted onto the front door of more agencies than Italy has had governments, the new-business pitch should be broken down as follows:

▪ Showreel of ads done for others:	10 mins
▪ Reiteration of the client's brief:	10 mins
▪ Research:	10 mins
▪ His strategy to interpret brief based on the research (ie the proposal itself):	30 mins
▪ Questions:	15–30 mins
TOTAL	1 hour 30 mins

But what of the audience?

Audience attitude

You have a captive audience, and this is undoubtedly a serious occasion, although it doesn't have to be that formal: the two are not mutually exclusive. But nevertheless, kneecaps will turn to jelly because you – the pitcher – know one thing: you stand to win what could be substantial income in a performance lasting just a couple of hours at most.

Wow! Just two hours – the time it takes to shower, dress and breakfast in the morning, or to drive down Piccadilly in rush-hour London – and you and your company could be popping champagne corks, thanks to the promise of your prospect-turned-client's money swelling your bank account.

Or you could be glumly contemplating the bloody 'three W's': what went wrong! There's a new element here, best described as *sweaty*. Why? Because if you foul up, you'll not only lose your dignity, as you would in a TV studio, conference hall or ballroom: you'll also, in this case, lose the opportunity of a potential fortune, into the bargain!

And that's what makes the new business pitch so challenging. It's what also makes it uncanny and unreal. You know that the prospect knows that you stand to swell your bank account if you win. And you also know that the prospect knows that it's in his gift. So what attitude should you adopt?

If you're too sycophantic, your prospect will quickly lose respect for you. If, on the other hand, you overcompensate the other way and become arrogant, that will also score against you. The truth is that pitchees hate fawning obsequiousness in their pitchers as much as they do aggressive bumptiousness.

So the answer? It has to be the middle route. Be relaxed rather than formal, succinct rather than verbose, firm rather than aggressive, and confident rather than submissive. A difficult course to steer? Yes, but being aware of it is the first step to 'solving' it.

So to conclude – environment matters, and you must tailor your performance to suit the occasion.

But there's one single aspect that is common to all occasions, all environments. It will be vital whether you're in a radio interview, or socking it to them at a new business pitch in a conference or at an after-dinner speech.

What is it? It's all to do with *confidence*. And it's what we examine next in Chapter 6 on preparing for the pitch itself.

WHAT HAVE WE LEARNT?

- How you need to tailor your performance to suit the timeframe of your pitch, and its different audience.
- Why you need to get your key points across sometimes in only 15 seconds in a radio/TV interview.
- Why conference audiences are captive – and expectant, because they've parted with ready money to hear you.
- Why the first five minutes of an after-dinner speech is the most vital, in branding you a success or failure.
- How anecdotes can signal the difference between a joke and a serious point.
- How to steer a middle course between being relaxed rather than formal, firm rather than aggressive, confident rather than submissive, succinct rather than verbose.

6 PREPARING TO PITCH

(HOW TO OVERCOME THE WOBBLIES AND GAIN CONFIDENCE IN MIND AND BODY BY A SET OF SIMPLE TRICKS)

In which we learn:

- Why it's pointless to speak.
- Why the confidence shield has nothing to do with teeth, and how it can help you overcome fear in mind and body.
- All about physical codes and the psychological tricks of non-verbal communication.
- The difference between you as a snapshot and as a moving picture.
- How toast and coffee can put you on the right scent.
- How to juggle dominance with submission.
- How to use hand signals and to master blunder recovery, and create space and drama.

Most people who go into a pitch of some sort are fearful of the event. Most, too, are ashamed to admit even to themselves that their stomach has developed into something resembling a jelly baby. But they shouldn't. It's normal.

No one is immune from nerves, to one degree or another – and, what's more, this should be viewed positively, not negatively. It's actually a necessary ingredient of a good performance!

I've always believed in adrenalin as a beneficial liquid when it is eagerly pumped through our bodies to stoke us up into the right frame of mind (and body) for us to be able to win: alert and excited, just like animals in the jungle when they are faced with a not-too-dissimilar fight for survival (OK you don't look like a wildebeest, and you're not going to be eaten alive – not literally, anyhow).

Are you telling me actors don't get nervous before going on stage;

that newscasters don't get the jitters, cabinet ministers – or even the clergy – goose bumps? Of course they do – so you are in pretty damn good company.

THEIR WINNING WAYS: DAVID WHITAKER

(Chairman of J Whitaker & Sons, publishers of *Whitaker's Almanack*, amongst others.)

I met the charming and urbane Mr Whitaker at a dinner party given by an ex-client, John Cooper. As a well-known after-dinner speaker, David and I soon got talking about the confidence issue, and he told the following story about a publishing colleague André Deutsch and the inimitable actor, Sir Lawrence, later Lord, Olivier. He said:

> André was in the Festival Hall theatre, because he was associated with a charity event to be held there, when he suddenly saw Lord Olivier on the stage – trying it out for a future event. Although the theatre was empty, André was concerned because he thought the great Lawrence Olivier looked unwell. As he, Olivier, came down off the stage he seemed to trip slightly and Deutsch grabbed his hand to steady him.

David continued:

> André was shocked to find that Olivier's palm was wet with sweat and so enquired whether he was alright. Then came the reply from the great man – no, he wasn't unwell, he was a trifle nervous.
>
> 'Nervous?' said André, with incredulity – 'But there's no one here in the theatre, Mr Olivier.' Whereupon came the reply: 'But there is you, dear boy.'

Which goes to prove beyond doubt, that if even Lord Olivier can admit nervousness in an empty theatre, why should we worry?

I was also told once by a not unattractive woman who understandably wishes to remain anonymous, that she would go into a pitch that day without wearing knickers! Odd, yes. But why? Because it simply gave her a degree of confidence in the knowledge that she knew something they didn't! Ah well, each to their own, and all that: but do you have an off-beat way of gaining confidence? If so, please write to me, Quentin Bell, c/o Kogan Page, 120 Pentonville Road, London N1 9JN. I'll award a bottle of champagne to the best ten to come in.

There are ways and means that skilled people use to overcome their fears, and so should you. They fall into two categories; we will touch on them both now. One is physical (dress code) and the other psychological (body code). They both highlight the importance of visual factors.

THE PHYSICAL CODE, AND WHY THE VISUAL MATTERS

It may seem bizarre to say it, but *speaking* at a pitch is a pretty pointless, even futile exercise.

Why? Because according to various pieces of research, as much as 95 per cent of the messages we initially pick up from other people are visual. And that means quite simply that the pitchee's *eye* is the primary antenna, not the *ear*. It's the eye that feeds that vital initial information to our brain in order for us to make judgements of others; those snap decisions that form our first opinions – probably in a microsecond.

ASIDE

Think of the last time you said: 'He/she was a fabulous speaker, but wait a minute, I can't remember an awful lot that was said.' Don't worry, you're not alone: it's quite common. But it doesn't say a lot for our mental agility as a species. Just think of all those totally wasted speeches taking place forlornly across the world each day that fall on stony ground and thus become pointless . . . wow!

Remember, too, that the world was created in such a manner as to cause us (everybody) the maximum distraction. So when you sit down as a delegate at a conference or seminar, the last thing you will be allowed to do is to concentrate on the *speaker*.

Why? Because there'll be a waiter asking about – or spilling – the wine. A colleague whispering in your ear. A delegate at the next table dropping a knife on the floor. A man hilariously but unwittingly dropping cigar ash down a female guest's voluptuous cleavage, on whom your eyes are transfixed . . . and so on.

So, when you do turn to the speaker, poor sod, you've missed half his/her major points and you concentrate on the visual. 'That's an odd tie, or dress', you think – she doesn't look much like her media photograph, or when she's been on TV.

Which isn't to say, of course, that although the odds do seemed to be stacked against us from the start, we shouldn't attempt to speak even if all the evidence points to its futility. But it does highlight the need for us all to be aware of the importance of those personal visual images – physical and psychological – that we transmit to the outside world.

Think of the last time you were on a crowded train (and which train isn't crowded?). You may not have picked up *exactly* what the couple were saying in the seat opposite, but you were fascinated, were you not, with them both: the way they talked, moved, giggled, gasped.

And it's precisely because we find others so fascinating that I believe everyone should try (metaphorically speaking) to *stand above themselves* and look down (even if one might spy a bald patch, in my case).

That might seem a daft thing to say, but I've always felt most of us are too inward-looking, in the sense that we don't endeavour to see ourselves as other see us. We might look into the mirror every day – but I bet we all subconsciously strike the pose that we want to see, not the real one others observe.

Think about it! Because we are all slaves to our egos to one degree or another, we will all wish to see our *best side*: tummy pulled in, cheeks hollowed . . . how many of us can hand-on-heart say we are not sullied by such trivia? Not many, is my guess.

■ ■ ■ ■ ■ ■ ■ ■ ■ ■ ■ ■ **FT Number 22** ■ ■ ■ ■ ■ ■ ■ ■ ■ ■ ■ ■

The truth is we, as people, are not snapshots – we are moving pictures: the snapshot pose we strike in front of a mirror does not often accord with the moving picture others see of us. So we must examine how we appear to others, in order to make the best of our pitch.
■ ■

Just think of the shock you had last time someone played back a video of you at a party. Or when you gasped with horror at an old photograph. Did I *really* look like that?. Do I *really* look like this? Probably, poor wretch.

The fact is we all conform to an appearance 'code of conduct', often without realising it. Thus, most lawyers and accountants will still dress in pin-stripe suits and brogue shoes, whilst some admen still wear double-breasted suits and loafers, with a roll-neck sweater making a tie redundant. And so, too, do the training shoe/baseball hat/T-shirt brigade conform to their own dress code, whilst believing themselves to be different. (Like all other 'tribal' dress codes they are, of course, conforming to a group ethos, as much as rebelling from any other.)

Whatever you wear, one thing is sure; it's your uniform, just like the ones our armed forces wear, only different. But what should you wear? Here's another FT with my advice:

■■■■■■■■■■■■ **FT Number 23** ■■■■■■■■■■■■

Choose whatever uniform you think your audience will be most comfortable with in relation to your type of audience and its expectation. Because you'll be comfortable then, too'.
■■■

So, even though you may be a transvestite at weekends, don't shock your audience and shatter their expectations by wearing your best frock to the pitch, even though you may love both the pattern and cut. Keep to the innate values that are yours but move down, or up, in appearance to suit (forgive the pun) the occasion. If not, you'll simply be out of kilter. (The day we pitched for a major agrochemical company I turned up in Barbour jacket and Hunter wellies. Well, the event was held in a marquee in a field, rather than an office, so I had an excuse!)

Above all, be smart. Even casual clothes are impressive when they're casual-smart, and that's the way I prefer to dress (no, not in a frock, thank you). I tried to give up the daily suit years ago, preferring to mix and match interchangeable trousers and jackets, and often in summer, no jacket – just shirt, tie, trousers. Why sweat my way to the office in a jacket, only to leave it hanging off the back of a chair all day, and then to wear it again on the sweaty journey home?

THE PSYCHOLOGICAL CODE

Meeting visual expectations concerns more than just dress, of course. Your confidence rating will be your most noticeable feature: pitchees are adept at smelling fear, and will delight at the prospect of tasting your blood on the podium or in the board room. So don't give them a chance. How?

QB'S CONFIDENCE SHIELD

By using my confidence shield, that's how – and I'm not talking about the state of your gnashers. (Remember that TV ad campaign for a toothpaste that featured the ring of confidence?)

No, I'm talking about a personal, invisible shield. Let me explain. Years ago I was terrified, like most, about entering a crowded room to pitch, especially in formal circumstances. The very thought of it sent me wobbly. My legs were made out of chewing gum, and my slip-ons felt heavy with all the blood that had drained into them from my face.

And then I invented the invisible shield. It enabled me to convince myself that I looked great (poor deluded fool), allowing me to hide behind that self-deception of my own making, so that all my wobbly bits (if you'll forgive the expression) were hidden from view. I realised, you see, that everyone in that room was actually just as nervous (or apprehensive) as I.

ASIDE

Remember the host or hostess of even a social party has every reason to be more shaky than the guests. She'll be obsessed with what happens if no one turns up, if the food's contaminated or if the wine's corked. She'll ask herself how she will remember the names of strangers in order to be able to introduce them to others. How will her reputation withstand such embarrassment? So don't you worry, you're a mere guest – you can relax. And so it is in a business pitch: the guests (your prospects) have the upper hand – it's you (like the hostess) that has all the work to do, both psychological and practical.

What exactly makes up the shield? It's basically a strong 'front' you can put out in order for people to judge you positively.

It's made up of five things (see Figure 7):

1. straight back and outstretched arm (to shake hands);
2. lingering eye contact;
3. smile;
4. question;
5. raised eyebrows.

Sounds trite? Maybe – but I found out then that if I walked into a room with the right 'entry language', to make me appear quietly confident,

The QB Confidence Shield

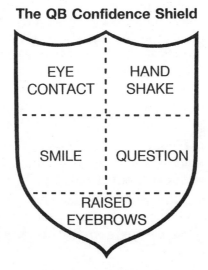

Figure 7 If you appear to be quietly confident at the outset, others will take you at that face value.

the audience accepted me instantly as quietly confident – and I thus gained that very quiet confidence.

I think you will, too. It's like a self-fulfilling prophecy.

ASIDE

On the first occasion that I used my shield, I made the mistake of far-too-hastily drinking two glasses of champagne which were eagerly thrust down my throat by waiters who gave the impression that unless they dispensed it from the bottle within seconds, it would corrode. The result was instant incoherance: so much for the shield! I was far too exhilerated by my successfully confident effort that I mistakenly let myself go. It was as if the alcohol had been on a hospital drip, straight into my bloodstream . . . and so, sadly, on this occasion, our hero (me) had to be led stumbling and bumbling into a taxi home. Ah well, we learn our lessons through experience. Remember: adrenalin needs only two glasses of bubbly alcohol to prove beyond scientific doubt that it is an embarrassingly potent mixture, especially on an empty stomach.

And now I make no excuses for paraphrasing an FT from another of my books, *The PR Business*, because it is entirely relevant.

■■■■■■■■■■■■ **FT Number 24** ■■■■■■■■■■■■

We are all in PR – sending out messages about ourselves every second of the day. And human nature being what it is, those messages will initially be accepted by others at their face value.
■■

And that's where the shield of confidence comes in. Because I was appearing confident, people accepted me on face value as confident – and I became it. How?:

- the confident handshake, with a fully outstretched arm pointed at the key person, as I walked towards him or her into the room;
- the lingering eye contact;
- the smile.

All these conspired to give out a message that said: 'I'm taking the intiative, and I'm very, very pleased – genuinely – to meet you.' (And that's exactly true – I am pleased: I stand to make money out of it, don't I, if I win the pitch?)

But there are two further items: the question and the raised eyebrows.

The question

Let's look first at the question, which is designed to give you the initiative whilst at the same time putting others at their ease.

It can be as simple as 'How do you do?', or 'Have you been to our part of London before?'; or 'Did you have trouble with the traffic?', or 'May I call you Darren?' (see Top Tip number 20). Whatever the question, what it actually does is very clever, and useful:

- it breaks the ice;
- it puts the onus on them to talk, not you;
- it puts both parties at their ease;
- it demonstrates that you have quietly (ie not agressively) taken the initiative.

I firmly believe that the very first question, asked in the opening minutes of a business relationship, can set the tone for the future.

The eyebrows

And the final one is the raised eyebrows. Try an experiment. Next time someone is talking to you, raise your eyebrows to denote anticipation (see Figures 8a and 8b). I bet they will follow suit and do the very same thing.

Figure 8a The author demonstrates his classic 'How do you do it?' routine. Raised eyebrows provide an ideal non-verbal binding.

Figure 8b The author shows the second sequence: 'I'll tell you.'

Why? Because they have clocked the fact you are openly interested in what is being said, and are flattered by it. So they reciprocate. It's a perfect piece of non-verbal communication.

So, when your client-prospect is replying to your question, or making a point of his own – raise your eyebrows at a pertinent point – normally at the end, but sometimes during his story. It'll provide a bond, so that the chances are you will be instantly liked (initially, anyhow) without the prospect knowing exactly why.

But there are other tips to help you through those vital first few minutes, when first impressions count.

YOUR OFFICE RECEPTION

One tip is the prospect's logo in your reception, should they be visiting you, with their personal names on it: 'Welcome to Ms Bigbudget of Sackyou plc', and such like. It flatters people – although I accept some may find it a bit false, or even sickly. But on the whole it does show your prospect that you value the opportunity of meeting them, and that can't be bad.

We at QBO once had a wedge-shaped office in Monmouth Street, in London's Covent Garden. The building looked enormous from the outside, but it was an illusion, because it tapered back fairly swiftly to almost nothing at the back. 'Just like a PR firm,' we jested nervously at the time, 'all front and no depth.'

The building also had a small, awkwardly-shaped reception area. The walls were built at drunken angles to each other, but we lined it from top to bottom with mirrors, in order for the area to appear bigger. The trouble was we found that in order to have a 'welcome' logo properly visible it had to be drawn *backwards* – a problem that threw our design department firstly into laughter and then subsequently despair. The reflections of one walled mirror to another were such that artwork showing a normally drawn client logo and message would be reflected backwards! So we had to compensate by drawing it the other way, if you get my drift . . . .

Despite the bizarreness of it, we found that this little quirk provided a talking point between us and the client, breaking that proverbial ice. Some even asked to take home the reversed logo as a souvenir.

THE SMELL OF BREAKFAST

Toast and coffee can help, too. At one time during the thrusting 1980s we used to have pitches before eight o'clock in the morning – a time of day I now hate for such intense physical exertion (I now devote all my energies at that time to the task of getting up and becoming accustomed to the day).

One thing that always seemed to endear us to our prospects was the alluring scent of fresh coffee, hot toast and warm croissants.

We soon realised that smell is a highly effective influence – arguably second after visual contact, and certainly up there.

So what did we do? We actually put a fan in the kitchen which, situated beside the reception, blew the alluring smells in the faces of our prospects. Don't laugh – I know it sounds pathetic – and I'm in no way suggesting a croissant will win you a pitch. But I am serious in pointing to a fact of life: if you link in to sub-conscious animal senses then you'll be doing yourself a favour.

SECRET SIGNALS

Given the importance of first impressions, what other tips and tricks can we learn to help us make the situation positive in preparing for the pitch? Learning to understand secret signals – like raised eyebrows – is one. Many people fail to appreciate the significance of the unspoken word – either through fear, modesty or ignorance.

For the truth is that we all can adopt and benefit from a series of existing signals – not dissimilar to morse code in wartime, flashing lights at sea or puffs of smoke used by Red Indians. If you can interpret these signs then you have a powerful weapon in your armoury which just *could* tip the balance between winning and losing a pitch. They are that important.

Let me give you an example. Imagine you're interviewing two people for a job. Without a word passing their lips, you can pick up hints about their characters.

John hovers at the door before coming in. He doesn't look you in the eye. His handshake is limp, only coming after you proffer your hand. As he sits (without being asked), he stares down at the table. His head remains still and his face expressionless as you explain about the job. His eyes display his nervousness, but this transmits as boredom to the onlooker. Everything about him shouts 'submissive' or 'disinterest', even though this may be far from the truth in reality. It's just that he hasn't learnt to see himself as others see him.

Sarah, on the other hand, appears at the door with a confident, honest grin. It's not the sort of smirk that could be misinterpreted as mischievous or disrespectful. She proffers her hand, her arm outstretched, and expresses interest in meeting me. When she sits, silently, her face is a classic in non-verbal communication. She nods to demonstrate an understanding of my point. Her eyebrows are raised to feign agreement. Her whole demeanour is one that speaks to me without words: she is alert, bright and interested, but not sycophantic or aggressive.

Who gets the job? You tell me. Like it or not, studies have revealed that, when it comes to judging a candidate's suitability, academic qualification or commercial experience is no panacea and may not be as persuasive as simple body signals. In other words, it's not just what you know – it's how you deliver it that counts.

And so it is with the pitch: if, for example, you are asked an unexpected question by the boss man, don't register disinterest in your face or by your actions – even if, yes, he is invoking a tedious golfing story, or one about his wife. Raise your eyebrows in anticipation, nod in the interim and smile in conclusion.

PRESENCE AND CHARISMA CAN BE LEARNT

Presence is an oft-used word. But what does it mean? My confidence shield can help, but we all know when someone walks into a room with that 'extra something' that makes people turn. It can be dismissed as a solely physical attribute, like height, but it is normally only an additional benefit. Make no mistake – people are not often born with charisma already built-in: it can be *learnt*. (Just like pitching can itself be learnt – see FT Number 1, Chapter 1.)

Small people can be very charismatic – and indeed often are the most so, because they have tried hard to overcome what they perceive to be a physical disadvantage. No, when you enter the pitch room, you are in a jungle, and what you must do is match the imagery you put out to the particular occasion, to the particular (or most important) person and to suit the mood.

You must, through the way you enter (and 'fill') the room show by your posture that you are important too, because as I've illustrated by the shield, confidence is catching: that's 'presence' in its purest form. But it can work against you. If you're too dominant where confidence is overtaken by perceived arrogance, then your prospect will feel threatened and you might as well forget the pitch.

DOMINANCE OR SUBMISSION?

Learning the delicate balance between dominance and submission is dependent on experience. But simply being aware of how much these things matter is 90 per cent of the battle, I believe.

Looking down on yourself in an imaginary way can help to balance the two – dominance and submission. You can demonstrate your confidence and presence when entering the pitch room and introducing yourself; then switching to a degree of submission in order to allow the boss of your prospect company to 'dominate' you, even for just a while. Don't fall into the trap of violating their space, or the fuses will blow and you'll have lost not just the initiative, but the pitch as well.

■■■■■■■■■■■■ **FT Number 25** ■■■■■■■■■■■■

Clever people recognise that it is not a weakness to appear submissive on the right occasion, provided you remain assured. To do so allows your opposite number – the prospect boss – to take the lead, and he or she will thus think more highly of you for this. If you are liked, you're more likely to win. Being a good listener is an example of this in action.

■■

Hand signals to endorse, underline or provide pitch-milestones are also vital, in my view.

We are all familiar with how the Prince of Wales splays out his hands before him when making a point. We may snigger at it, because it has become the repertoire for impressionists. But what do you do with your hands? How can you turn them into an active benefit? We'll examine later how visuals can become a focal point, but there are two particular hand signals I have always favoured.

CREATING SPACE AND DRAMA

Heaven knows what a psychologist might say about me, but I have found hand signals useful in two ways: they create space, and they create drama. Here's an example of how I would use them. I call it the 'How do you do it . . .?/I'll tell you' routine (see Figures 8a and 8b).

The outstretched arms (How do you do it?)

I am asking a question. It's rhetorical and I'm not expecting an answer – because I intend to give it myself.

Imagine you are in a law firm, and you are pitching for the contractual legal work for a major firm. You know the prospect is concerned about certain loopholes in his existing contracts. It threatens him. So you say – with your arms splayed widely: 'How do you go about plugging such a loophole, without drawing your customer's unwarranted attention to it?' You ask the question slowly in order to highlight and savour the question – and it is the hand gesture that helps you do it, by dictating how much 'space' (or silence) you leave between the words.

Drama is created further as you pause, silent, with each hand temporarily locked in the outstretched position. That links you into part two of the sequence.

The pointed finger (I'll tell you)

You have posed the question that you will know from your pre-pitch research is one that is vexing your potential client. But you don't wait for a cocky client prospect to chip in by saying, 'That's what I hoped you'd tell me.' You bring your arms back to the central position and, raising one hand with the finger pointing upwards (not accusingly at them) you say, again slowly, with your eyes locked on to those of your prospect-boss (who by now is hopefully in an ecstasy of anticipation): 'I'll tell you how . . . .'

Of course, you have to *know* how, even if you then go on to suggest how you find out what you don't yet know (ie you give them a critical path plan of how to go about it). I have found this technique has been very useful in the past, mainly because those physical movements allow you to space out your words and phrases to more dramatic effect. Practice it before your next pitch.

TALK LIKE A SNAIL, NOT A HARE

Most people talk too quickly. It's all to do with that 'winning fluid' I described earlier – adrenalin. Because its function is to help you leap through the jungle at a rate of knots sufficient to avoid becoming dead meat, it makes your system work extra fast, so you're extra alert to danger.

I guess that's what happens in a pitch situation: it's also a jungle. But because you're firing on all 48 valves, you also speak too fast. To you, in your intense state of jitters, you are possibly talking 'normally' – trying desperately to cover up the possibility of any embarrassing pause or silence. Horror of horrors, *silence*! In a pitch!

But actually, to a prospect sitting bemusedly sipping his coffee, or a delegate in an auditorium, you are 'gabbling' – tripping over your words and in danger of verging into incoherence.

So slow down. Be extra slow. Learn to love the pause. Work at it. Give light and shade to words and phrases. Learn to stretch words (see Chapter 7). Don't be afraid of a pause – use it to best effect. To you it may seem an eternity, but to your audience it won't be noticed (because their adrenalin isn't putting them into a hyper state, like you).

■■■■■■■■■■■■ **FT Number 26** ■■■■■■■■■■■■

By working at talking extra slowly you will end up only speaking normally – by compensating for the speed. And what's more, the little silences can greatly help your audience to digest what you've said. So not only will speaking extra slowly render you coherent, it'll improve communication and therefore understanding.

■■

BLUNDER RECOVERY

We all make blunders. By saying the wrong word, forgetting a word. Jumbling two or three together. But how do you extricate yourself from such an embarrassment? I'll tell you what I do, but first: let's examine why I use the word 'embarrassment'.

It's because, if you make a blunder, the horror can throw you into turmoil throughout the rest of the pitch. Put you off your stroke. Unless, that is, you stop and correct it, there and then. Don't lumber on! How? Pause after your gaff, look the prospect in the eye and say something like:

'Wait a minute, I'll say that again, with my teeth in this time.'

What'll it do? It'll change their potential embarrassment *for you* into a sympathetic admiration *of you*. That's because you recovered your composure by giving yourself extra time *and* made them smile – it's an ideal blunder-recovery mechanism. And it puts them on your side.

I don't believe it is in any way naff to practice all these little tricks in front of your bedroom mirror well before the pitch. It can only help. So, too, can speaking into a tape recorder at different speeds. When you play yourself back you'll soon appreciate the importance of silence, and pace.

So, don't feel embarrassed, practise. Because it is far better to make your mistakes in your bedroom than in the real-life pitch environment.

And that's what we look at next : the real life event and my top tips for the pitch.

WHAT HAVE WE LEARNT?

- That everyone suffers from nerves, and that adrenalin is good for you.
- How to use a set of simple tricks to overcome your fear:
  - QB's Confidence Shield: outstretched arm, eye contact, smile, question, eyebrows routine;
  - The 'How do you do . . ./I'll tell you' routine.
- The importance of the visual – eye comes before ear, so dress code and body language are important to suit the occasion.
- The benefit of trying to see yourself as others see you – not just as you prefer to be!
- How being properly qualified for a job doesn't mean you'll get it, if you're not presenting yourself properly in the 'chemistry' department.
- How to recover from a blunder with a rehearsed quip to give yourself time and to put them on your side.
- How to learn to speak extra slowly, in order not to gabble.

7 TOP TIPS FOR THE PITCH PART ONE

PITCH EXECUTION: WHAT PHYSICAL ACCOUTREMENTS?

How to benefit from audio and visual support – from the simple to the complex; to create a framework and other structural 'prompts'.

So here we are. The day has arrived. No more theory – this is for real. But what do you do, apart from throw up in the loo? Here's what you do, summarised as follows in a 23-point Top Tips For The Pitch checklist for you to refer back to again and again.

When you boil it all down, there are only two little items to this pitching caper. One is the content; the other is execution.

And that's why I've divided these top tips into these two distinct sections. Whilst there will be some overlap, here part one deals with all the necessary (or if not necessary, then desirable) physical accoutrements like audio-visual support techniques, prompts and structure. Part two, beginning on page 110 is focused more on to pitch content, and thus *what* you say and *how* you say it.

TOP TIP

NUMBER 1

USE OF VISUAL SUPPORT TECHNIQUES

Conventional wisdom has it that it is confusing to be harangued by both verbals and visuals at the same time. The inference is that verbal assault is good enough. Nonsense!

Visuals can help in two ways:

1. They help your audience visualise the point you're making and thus better digest it.

2. They help *you* structure your own pitch talk, by enabling you to use the visuals as vital prompts to tell you it is time for the next 'verbal'.

The second point is often largely overlooked, because most people like to write lashings of notes – a sure death, as we'll see shortly. So why not make up your slides or acetates with headlines that sequentially walk you through your own argument? I do.

But there are dangers. Badly done visuals – whether in the form of 35 mm slides, acetates for overhead projectors, or some of the more high-tech options discussed in Top Tip Number 12 – can serve to confuse, rather than to enhance.

ENHANCE, DON'T COMPLICATE

One of the biggest traps we human beings fall into is to over-complicate: instead of using a couple of key words, a phrase or a visual picture to *enhance* the point being made (and to act as a prompt for the presenter) they achieve precisely the opposite. This happens when something is up on screen that conflicts with what is being said, or is too long and cumbersome to be immediately understood.

Your audience, probably not gifted with the best (brains or) eyesight, will squint at your lavish text-ridden slides, desperately trying to read them. But they cannot – least of all because when talking you are stupidly using different words to those on the slide. It's a recipe for disaster, I fear.

■ ■ ■ ■ ■ ■ ■ ■ ■ ■ ■ ■ **FT Number 27** ■ ■ ■ ■ ■ ■ ■ ■ ■ ■ ■ ■

Remember, most mortals cannot walk and chew gum at the same time – which means that if you show a slide with visuals that differ even slightly from what is coming out from your mouth, then you'll only succeed in blowing all the fuses in your audience's minds. People cannot hear and see easily at the same time if you mean them to understand as well. So, visuals must enhance your verbal assault, not scupper it.

■ ■

REVEALING THE 'REVEAL'

You should try to pace yourself when you use an OHP, to stop your audience reading *all* your headlines at once. What's the point of you concentrating on the top message on your acetate when you are allowing them to read on to the next parts below? It'll again confuse – but there is a solution: the famous 'reveal' technique. What is that when it's at home? It's an age-old method of placing sheets of paper across the bottom of your text so that only the top parts you are referring to on screen are visible. You move the 'mask' downwards as you proceed, thus controlling the speed at which they move on, too.

CREATING A MOOD

Your visuals do not *just have* to be simply a *written* 'headline' distillation of what you are saying. A photograph or drawing can also be used to create a mood to illustrate and enhance your point.

For example, on the various occasions that I give talks on PR to those rash enough to pay for the privilege, I illustrate the point that all of us are 'in PR', whether we like it or not, by showing colour slides of different people's shoes (see Figure 9).

My argument is that – cost notwithstanding – we don't simply buy shoes to keep our feet from the ground. We choose the style and type to portray an image of ourselves. Why else would there be so many styles and types from which to choose, from the ubiquitous trainers and Doc Martins to boots and highly polished Oxfords and brogues?

Instead of the 'shoe slide' I could have put up a slide that said in a typeface of my choice:

- The shoes-choice represents the fact that we are all in PR; we have no choice whether we present ourselves in one way or another to others.
- So, it follows that if we have to present ourselves anyway why not present our *best*, most appropriate face?
- For how we are viewed by others depends on how we present ourselves to them.
- We will be accepted by others at face value.
- The need to 'manage' our communications well is something both people and companies have in common if we want to 'be successful'.

But I didn't, feeling that the shoe illustration would better replace the ninety-odd words, and thus project my point more easily. What did it do? It created a mood which simply communicated an otherwise complex and long verbal slide.

In general, it's important to remember that the successful combination of 'visual and verbal' can become a fantastic communications force: the sum of the two together is far more effective than the individual parts themselves.

Furthermore, the written report you leave behind after the pitch – including visuals such as the shoe slide and graphs, etc – will reawaken the positive memories gained in the pitch and thus, by rights, should

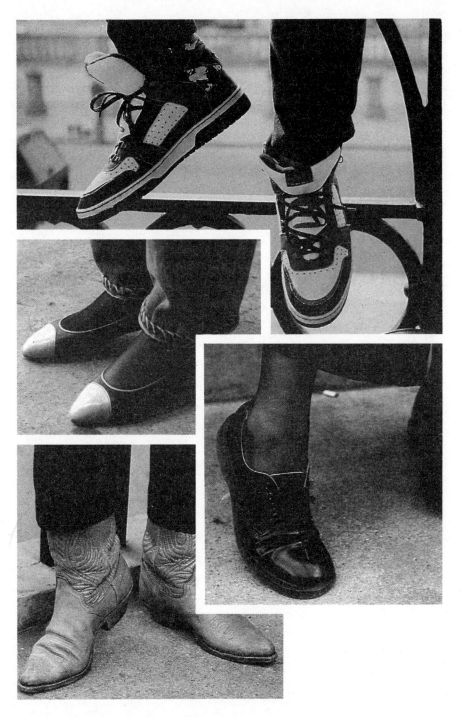

Figure 9 It's their difference that they have in common.

place you and your pitch team in a pole position. You are, after all, making an attempt to communicate simply, effectively and 'emotionally'.

Emotion is the key. Think of the difference between a love letter and a letter from the Inland Revenue. Both lie unopened on your doormat. Both will invoke strong associations in your mind as you pick them up and as you are just about to open them – but in entirely different ways.

The love letter will be cherished, because even before you've torn apart the envelope your memory bank will open up and flood your consciousness with a myriad of pleasant thoughts, rekindling many a warm experience. And so too will the other unopened letter from Her Majesty – rekindle memories, that is, but not necessarily ones you will relish – especially if, as is most likely, it's a demand for payment.

So what am I driving at? An audio tape of a great orator like Sir Winston Churchill is able to immediately invoke visuals of the great man in your mind, merely by hearing his voice. And not just of him – it is also more than likely to paint a picture of the time: a wartime living room with a family listening intently around an open fire to a bakelite radio uttering one of his wartime speeches.

Now, whether you are actually old enough to have been there at the time, or have seen such a scene portrayed in a TV play, or on film, is irrelevant. What is important is that a strong visual is inextricably linked in your mind to a voice. It's a powerful duo – the visual and the verbal – if done properly.

Arguably the greatest (certainly the most enduring) book ever written – the Bible – relies on parables that create visuals in people's minds in order to make a particular point – even though, paradoxically, it contains no actual visuals or photographs. But you, by use of your visuals can attempt to place memories in your audience's minds that they'll take away with them.

So the clever use of illustrative visuals (like the shoes) can be a highly powerful way of supporting the mood of your messages, and a method of rocketing you and your team above your competitors. How do you tell which visuals are likely to be good, and which bad? That's Top Tip Number 2.

TOP TIP

NUMBER 2

VISUALS: THE GOOD, THE BAD (AND SOMETIMES UGLY!)

Telling which visuals are likely to be good and which bad is damned difficult, I can tell you, and only comes with experience. There are guidelines to be followed, however, and they follow here. Good visuals should fall into one of the following three categories:

1. text, in headline form;
2. graphics;
3. visual illustrations (eg photograph or drawing).

To summarize, here is a brief rationale as to why it may be foolhardy *not* to use one or more of these three basic formats. We've covered the visual type – photographs, drawings or illustrations – so here's text and graphics.

TEXT

Keep it simple. Don't fall into the trap of writing long explanations, because – as we've learnt – your audience won't be able to read whilst you talk – and take both in. Moreover, the fewer words you use, the *bigger* and more powerful they can be made on screen (see Figure 10).

Figure 10 The *bigger* the words on screen, the more impact they have.

The converse is also true: the more wordy your slide becomes, the smaller and less effective the text will become. You'll thereby fail in two ways (a double whammy): your audience will accept it as a challenge of Anneka Rice proportions to attempt to read text which is presented as though it has been written by a demented spider. They'll fail, and in so doing they'll actually miss what you subsequently said into the bargain.

■■■■■■■■■■■■ **FT Number 28** ■■■■■■■■■■■■

Learn to write in headlines. Pick one word or phrase that encapsulates what you are about to say, even if you have to follow with a couple of subheadings that qualify or further explain your point.

■■

GRAPHICS

Kept simple, graphic charts still reign supreme as a method of concisely demonstrating a point. Here are examples of some of the graphics I've used (see Figure 11):

- pie charts/bar charts;
- flow charts/critical path analyses;
- circles;
- inverted and upright triangles.

They by no means have to be restricted to financial or market share information, as some suppose. What can be put into a graphic format is really only limited by your imagination.

An inverted triangle, for example, is one we at QBO have used over the years – and to some success. It can be adapted, chameleon-like, to numerous situations: the one illustrated demonstrates how the PR discipline can dovetail into a prospect's marketing mix, to show that is has a distinct and valuable role. Naturally, having established PR's saliency as a discipline, we then went on to describe why we were the best PR firm to carry out a campaign for the client. Couldn't you adopt this technique to your own business? I'm sure you could.

For more on the use of pitch equipment, see also Top Tip numbers 12 (latest technology available) and 15 (change of equipment for light and shade).

TOP TIP

NUMBER 3
BUILD IN MILESTONES

Imagine you're going on a car journey to meet a friend in a part of the world unfamiliar to you. Your friend says:

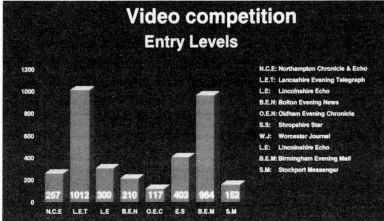

SUMMARY

Figure 11 Examples of some of the graphics used to make visual points.

'Turn right by the Church, go straight ahead over the mini roudabout, and turn left at the sex shop (don't waiver). You can't miss it.'

Well, in the same way that you need your church, your mini roundabout and sex shop to guide you on this particular journey, so too you need your milestones to direct your prospective client's attention through the various points on the journey that makes up your pitch. These points will be better made if they are in physical visual form.

Now, I've always been one that questions conventional wisdom in life, but there is one conventional wisdom which is gold-plated and which bears repeating here. It is a pitch formula that will always hold true. It is the most fundamental of milestones, the 'Great Three' paraphrased by me from the original. It is:

■ Tell the audience what you're going to tell them (that should effectively taken care of when – as described in Top Tip number 7 – you start at the end).
■ Tell them it (this will be the detail of the pitch itself).
■ Tell them again what you've told them (this will be a succinct reminder of what they heard, in order to square the circle).

In the first part of the above formula, you are providing milestones, giving your audience an indication of what to expect on the pitch journey.

One of the best ways to appreciate how successful such a formula can be, is to imagine yourself in your prospective client's underwear (so to speak): reverse the roles, in other words.

You, as a potential client don't know what to expect – so you need to be told. You need milestones, in short, to guide you through the maze so that there can be no misunderstandings.

So what do you say? It might go something like these hypothetical examples:

Milestone one

Good morning/afternoon. What we would like to demonstrate to you today is how a revitalised marketing programme [or it could be auditing procedure, or what have you] could, we believe, help you to increase your bottom line profitability by up to 20 per cent. In order to tell you how, our presentation will last one hour, following which we have allocated 30 minutes for questions.

Milestone two

First, however, we want to show you the research we've conducted in the market-place that has revealed what we believe to be a competitive opportunity for you to achieve just that type of growth.

Milestone three

This will be followed by our proposals, which will highlight how we we believe you should maximise on this opportunity, both strategically and tactically.

Milestone four

And finally, we will flag up notional budgets and indicate the timescales and people resources needed to accomplish it.

All four of these milestones should be put on slide or acetate in more succinct headline form whilst you go through each one. Alternatively, they could be presented on a 3 feet by 2 feet board that stays on an easel (or is propped up elsewhere) throughout the presentation, so there can be no doubt about what to expect in the running order. Naturally, however, you needn't use the word 'milestone', but can refer instead to the different stages or parts of your show.

Remember too, milestones can also act as an insurance policy: if during the presentation anyone rashly interrupts to ask whether you're going to cover one part or another – say budgets – you can bring back this milestone slide (or refer them to the board) to remind them what you said at the outset. (And shut them up!)

 NUMBER 4

THINK SUCCINCT WITH BOX NOTES

Attempting to make any pitch from memory is a task which is beyond 'Superpitcher', let alone the likes of you and me. So, if you aren't memory man or madam and you have *not* got physical visuals to prompt you as I described previously what prompt technique do you adopt? What can you do if you are about to stand up in front of 500 people at an after-dinner speech?

The prospect of holding reams of notepaper that shake so furiously in your nervous, sweaty palms that the ink smudges into an incomprehensible amorphous blur as they fall to the floor and are entirely out of order and upside down when you pick them up – to the embarrassment of all – is a horror not worth contemplating.

The answer lies in the use of boxed headlines on card files. But wait awhile, there's a catch. The trouble with getting acquainted with the box note system is that it goes against the grain. It's not natural. Why? Because it aims to simplify things – and humans don't like that. We like, by nature, to be fulsome rather than concise when it comes to the pitch.

So it is the most natural thing in the world to draft reams of complex notes when composing a speech where we know (like perhaps at a seminar, an impromptu goodbye drink to a valued employee, or the after-dinner talk) there will be no audio-visual support to act as a prompt.

We do this natually: our nervous system within us will ensure that, for fear of being rendered silent with no more to say on the night, we will over-compensate by drafting a speech of Churchillian proportions.

As we read it each time, we think of something else to add. 'I mustn't forget that bit', we mutter. But nothing could be worse, in fact. Why? Because of two factors.

1. Your long draft will be written (probably badly) as if it is to be read word-for-word. Heaven forbid!
2. The turgid text will perversely serve to camouflage the key points, that actually you should endeavour to highlight. They'll be in there somewhere, but will you be able to find them? Not on the night, I assure you, when your terror is at its peak and your concentration at its worst.

Let's examine this in greater detail, and find out why the box note system can help you to 'think succinct'. I've already said that the last thing you should aim for in any pitch is to read from long notes. Like woollen long-johns on a wedding night, the prospect will never serve to stimulate, and will only succeed in quashing any excitement in your audience. But why?

It'll lack any semblance of spontaneity, that's why. It's a potentially difficult trick, but what we must all learn to master is a delivery that appears spontaneous, and which – particularly in the case of an after-dinner speech – is also ten or twenty minutes packed with three or four poignant messages, sequentially linked and if possible entertainingly rendered. (Wow, is that all?, I hear you ask.)

But don't worry, help is at hand – and it comes, despite the initial difficulties you may experience in using them, in the form of the box note system. The great benefit of this system is that it becomes the very discipline you need to help you to extract, from the darkest corners of that sponge called your brain, the key points you want to put across.

Here's how you do it. Think of a maximum of three or four points. Not much eh? No – and that's precisely the point: the aim is to *reduce* the number of key points to be made. You have to overcome any natural instinct to waffle on. Francis Hallawell, QBO's director who runs our training division which arranges sessions in pitch and media training technique courses, and who is one of the UK's most skilful practitioners in his field, has coached a number of QBO's legal and chartered surveyor clients in the box system – professionals not always noted for their presentational prowess. He is almost visionary in his zeal to get these delegates to distil their speech into three or four key points, and then to produce sub-points under each.

When that's done, it's easy-peasy to stand up – glancing occasionally to the card for guidance. And if you can get all your boxes on *one* of those stiff filing cards, rather than two or three, all the better.

What you'll develop in using this technique is a greater admiration of your own memory bank, because you've only got to glance at the key word on the card to spark off a computer-like connection in your subconscious that will zap you to the next key point/s or descriptions which – without fail – will pop up in your mind, like a 35 mm slide out of a library. It won't let you down, believe me. But you have to put that trust to the test!

But why do I call it the box system? It's simply because I put all the key points in a box of their own, with a flow line between them. Let me give you an example, which also demonstrates how the technique can be used in radio interviews.

When I launched my last book I undertook some twenty such interviews, some on national and others on local radio. As you can see from my box notes (see Figure 12) I managed to get all my prompts on a single card, which was thus easily transportable via my pocket (no briefcase full of notepaper) into the studio. Even though I was the actual author of the book, I still needed this prompt to set the cogs in my mind whirling. Otherwise, it might have stayed totally fuzzy.

ASIDE

How can I be relied on to remember what I've already forgotten?' is an immortal line out of Joe Orton's play, *What the Butler Saw*, and I think it sums up how the mind is adept at going completely blank just when the pressure to remember is most intense.

Once triggered, I found my so-called memory box automatically spewed up the rest. You too can rely on the technique, I assure you – provided you keep those triggers simple. So what was my 'line of

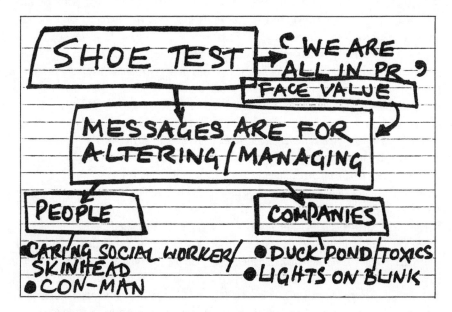

Figure 12 How to make the most of a single prompt card.

attack' triggered by the card? Why not, before reading on, study the box card illustration, and see if you can imagine how the interview might have gone. Here's a clue: it's an extension of my 'shoe' example given earlier.

This is what I actually would have said during the interview, over as much as 15 minutes. The prompts all came from an A6-sized card:

■ The fact that we all have a choice in the style and type of shoes we wear (my so-called 'shoe test') proves that we are all in PR: we have no choice. Shoes are not just for keeping our feet from the ground. They say something about us, our style and our personality.

■ We are thus all sending messages about ourselves every minute of the day – messages that will be initially accepted by others at face value. We should be aware of all this, as a fact of life.

■ We have the power to change all the images we send; messages are for altering – for managing – but very few of us wilfully and wittingly do so. Usually it is a common denominator of all successful people.

■ What applies to us as individuals also applies to corporations and companies.

■ Example (of us as people): you can't pretend to be a caring social worker if you look and dress like a skinhead, as you'll probably put the fear of God into everyone.

- Example (of us as a company): you can't claim to be an upstanding member of the community if you're actually pouring toxic acids down the village duck pond.
- Example (people): think how an expert conman can fool even the most cynical because they are taken at face value as being trustworthy.
- Example (company): think how a factory's fluorescent facia on the blink, dirty windows or a scruffy reception can give out a poor impression; if they care so little about their outward appearance, will their products or services be as sloppy? It's an association you're entitled to make.

That little description runs to over 270 words. Can you imagine carrying such notes into the studio when the heat is on? You'd fumble, to say the least.

The point I'm making? It's this: boil down your messages and put them into the box note system. That way you will trigger the brain into action by providing key 'entry signals',* like a computer. That's how the silicon chips work, after all.

TOP TIP

NUMBER 5
DISCARD GIMMICKS

There are some physical prompts you can do without. In the glorious days of the 1980s it was funky to get up to all sorts of gimmicky tricks in order to push home a point. But the trouble with all of that fun was that it became tedious. When *everyone* has a gimmick up their sleeve, you can say goodbye to innovation, as the message often becomes sublimated by the trick itself.

ASIDE

I once pitched to a major aluminium producer. The thrust of our message to them was that all the PR tactics had to link somewhere with the colour of aluminium: in other words the product was the message. So, in order to get this across I hired a model, dressed her in a scanty aluminium-coloured outfit and got her to leap on to the prospects' board-table and prance up and down to the music of 2001.

The following things happened, sequentially:

---

* See also 'Signals and anecdotes', Chapter 5.

- ■ The prospect was lost for words.
- ■ We were thrilled.
- ■ We didn't get the business.

I've since believed that nothing can replace a well-constructed, professionally executed 'normal' pitch, because gimmicks can take on a life of their own and become 'bigger' than the message. They can be sickly, too. I once sat in on an advertising agency pitch for a major international charity I was advising. The big chief of one top agency couldn't (or wouldn't?) turn up with his team – so instead he sent a specially made video of himself saying how much they wanted the business. But it would have been cheaper and less pompous to have come in person, I believe.

THEIR WINNING WAYS: PETER GUMMER, CHAIRMAN, SHANDWICK PLC

'No presentation is the best presentation', Peter Gummer, Chairman of Shandwick PLC, told me over lunch, and he made the point with his usual clarity. For the man that has built up one of the world's largest consultancies from nothing meant simply this: the less physically complicated the pitch, the better. To illustrate the point, Gummer tells the following story:

> In 1975 we were pitching for Lymeswold Cheese. We allowed ourselves to be self-indulgent – using 24 carousels in a multi-media presentation. Looking back I suppose subconsciously it made us feel that bit more confident and self-important, convincing ourselves we must be pretty damn good with such a sophisticated show. But it was disastrous – trying to get all those pieces of technology to work in a cohesive manner was a nightmare.
>
> But that wasn't the end of it. We had made a rather expensive model of the cheese *in ice* – as a gimmick, I suppose.
>
> Looking back, it seems bizarre that we didn't think of it in advance – but yes, the ice model gradually began to melt thanks to the heat of the technology and – I suspect – our own nerves. Finally, the whole thing toppled off the table and crashed down, just missing the client chairman. We didn't win the business.

It takes great style for Peter to recount such a story that lesser men might interpret as weakness. But we all learn from our mistakes, and to prove that humility does matter Shandwick has since never looked back and has became a world class leader in its field.

TOP TIP — NUMBER 6
TAKE SPONTANEITY SERIOUSLY

There is another physical prompt that is not often used extensively, but this time it's a human being. One of yours to be precise – an employee or colleague.

It's always a bad idea to enter a pitch with people from your outfit who don't say a single word. 'What are they doing there, wasting space?', a client is fully entitled to ask. So always give every member of your team a role – or show them the door. If there is no obvious, original role, make it one of 'amplification' support.

What do I mean by this? Simply that those who are without a major role can utter 'scripted asides' in order to amplify a statement made. This can be by way of illustration:

'What we did for client X in that situation, and it worked well for him, was to . . . .'

Or it can be to underline a point by approaching it in another way:

'Another way of looking at that particular point is to consider it the other way round. If we *don't* follow this route then we risk a competitor stealing our thunder . . . .'

Either way, treat such seemingly spontaneous remarks *seriously* – and rehearse doing it.

TOP TIP — NUMBER 7
START AT THE END

Stupid? No, it's rather as I suspect some of our fictional novelists (and I'm a budding amateur) act: they begin with an ending in mind. So should you, because by working out your structure in this way you'll also be providing a solid physical prompt mechanism for yourself to be guided by, or manoeuvred within.

As in Top Tip number 2, begin by saying: 'What we aim to demonstrate to you today is . . . [mention end result].' You can then jump backwards, in the sense that you can then sequentially justify how you've concluded that way. But what could the end be?

Well, it could be:

■ Why a new creative treatment of your current advertising can reach new consumers (if you're an advertising agency after their account).
■ Why there's a whole new business application for your product

that hasn't been exploited (if you're a marketing or management consultancy).

■ Why legal precedents will enhance your efforts in international acquisitions (if you're a legal firm specialising in that area).

■ Why you can solve their human resource problem in Albania by hiring a non-executive director in London (if you're a headhunter dealing in international searches).

■ Why your office design is both aesthetically pleasing and totally functional (if you're an architectural practice pitching for a new office complex).

And so on. Of course, the same can apply to matters of a more academic nature: one can easily imagine a scientist beginning at the end when describing his personal theory of how the universe started (although one hopes not literally at the end of the world). What he will do is to start at the end with his prognosis – and then go back to the beginning and build up his case.

Now, the last thing I'd want to do is to suggest that pitching is an academic exercise – far from it. But, as you will have gathered, where there is a sequential argument of the case ('sequential' is a term I'd rather use than 'logical' – I don't readily like to admit logical argument exists, in this context), then one can draw parallels.

ASIDE

If pitching isn't a logical process, then what is it? It's certainly not a science, because there are no 'laws' as such in my view – or certainly no laws that cannot be changed. No, pitching, like life itself, is a mixture of intuition, *emotion* and personality married to energy, *emotion* and ambition. Will that do?

But having started at the end (eg 'We want your business because,') how do you then successfully go back in order to make your case? That's Top Tip number 8.

TOP TIP   NUMBER 8

BUILD AROUND A CENTRAL THEME

Every pitch must have a theme, which effectively links all the 'arguments' you are putting forward, messages to be conveyed or points made.

Thus, when at QBO we were pitching for part of the TSB's business – a campaign aimed at the youth market – we came up with a research-based PR proposal that would survey the attitudes of young people twice: once before they left school on their aspirations of the great wide world of work outside, and the other a year later on what it was really like. To give it a pithy title we called it our 'Dreams and Reality' programme.

In this way the central theme represents the handle to help your prospective client pick up your case. Good ones will encapsulate, in a few simple words, the entire *essence* of what you're trying to say: such a theme will become the title of the pitch document you will leave with the client, and it may even appear on each of your audio-visual slides or acetates. It may, as we have done at QBO on numerous occasions, have its own special logo (see 'Dreams' pillow, Figure 13).

Figure 13 A pithy and memorable title can be used to encapsulate the essence of your pitch in two or three simple words.

TOP TIP **NUMBER 9**
ARTICULATE YOUR TEAM HIERARCHY

Make sure your audience know 'who's who' in your team right at the outset of the pitch. Don't rely on the fact they've been introduced when you arrived: no one will remember the names. Say: 'Before we start I'd just like to reiterate the team here today . . .'. Start at the bottom end, leaving yourself last – assuming you will be the top person, kicking off the proceedings. If possible, add drama by saying: 'All the people in this room today will be working on your business . . . .'

This will achieve two things:

■ It will impress the pitchees that what they see is what they will be buying. There'll be no 'passing down the pyramid' with the top guys never seen again once the business is secured, and only juniors handling all the important work.

■ More importantly, it'll provide the prospect with a clear understanding of the team hierarchy right at the outset, with complete transparency.

No reasonable client can expect the senior partner or managing director to do everything on his business. He can't expect – or even afford (as his hourly rates will be higher) – to be the subject of the MD's sole attention. So others in the team will have various responsibilities, depending on their seniority and the appropriate need.

But all this needs to be articulated – so grasp the nettle on this one right at the outset: say who will lick the stamps, do the admin, market research, day-to-day implementation and strategic direction (or whatever). It'll make your prospective client feel comfortable and cosy in the knowledge that you have given sufficient forethought to his every likely need or question. You've come across as a true professional. Let there be no ambiguity and – if the prospect likes you and the chemistry is right – you're likely to be 90 per cent of the way to securing a new client.

TOP TIP

NUMBER 10

PICK ON THE SMILER AND NODDER

Look on the audience as your partner, not your adversary. There are usually one or two 'smilers' and 'nodders' in an after-dinner audience. They'll make you feel better – but you have to survey the faces in your audience in order to spot them. And remember, the audience is an integral part of your show – they are part of the partnership. Viewing them in that way will provide you with the best of all pitch structures to see you through the ordeal.

But who are they? They're the ones who look at you attentively: the ones who often smile, or nod as you speak. If you're nervous, frightened or just plain terrified as you step up in front of your audience, a friendly face can become a welcome aphrodisiac. A friendly face is, in short, a godsend to calm your nerves and put you on an even keel.

But don't linger too long: as you become more confident, move your gaze across the audience, only homing-in on your 'friend' from time to time, for a top-up of reassurance. You mustn't give the constant impression that you're talking just to one person, however – staring at him or her alone will soon unnerve the person in question and upset the rest. If you gain eye contact with everyone in the audience from time to time, they'll all be flattered.

You'll also find a grim sod, or two. What do you do with them? Look'em in the eye too, I say. If they're a delegate learning from you at a seminar, ask them a question or two – if appropriate. In short, counter them head on – because often you'll find that they are grim-looking simply because they expect your talk to be a serious affair – or their expression may simply register their thoughtfulness, not their agression. Don't too readily assume that they're agin' you!

Either way, remember to gain eye contact right away with the most important people in the room – the audience on whom you will rely. Without them, you'd be wasting your time, so mentally 'pull them in' as part of the structure of the event. Let them prop you up. Don't, through nerves, allow a partnership 'cavern' to emerge right from the outset, or you'll be greatly impeding your chances of success.

■■■■■■■■■■■■ **FT Number 29** ■■■■■■■■■■■■

All pitches should be viewed as a partnership. Pitchees want you to succeed too, don't forget. They'll be right on your side at the outset – the last thing they want is an embarrassing charade.
■■■

TOP TIP

NUMBER 11

GO FIRST

Much debate has been conducted around the subject of the pitch 'slot'. If you are in a competitive situation and the prospect is devoting one whole day to be entertained by – say – four companies, where should you ask to be placed in the pitching order (if you have a choice)?

I would always say first, although there can be no magic formula that will relate a placing to a guarantee of success. But your slot can help.

Why first?

- Because you're fresh (it is probably 9.00 am).
- Because you're energetic (eager to get on with it).
- Because first impressions, it's true, are normally more enduring.
- Because you'll set the standard by which others will be judged: if you're good, your pitchees will use your performance as a benchmark by which to judge the others.

Robert Bean, head of advertising at BT (and an ex-ad agency man, so he sees life from both the client and agency perspectives) summed it up to me over lunch one day by saying:

> To you it's your big day, but to your prospective client it's simply Wednesday. And given it is likely your competitors will at least in part have covered the same ground as you during their pitch, he should hear it from you first. By the time it is 3.30 pm and the last pitch of the day, your prospect will be getting frayed at the edges by the same clichés or received wisdoms cropping up.

Which brings me to a related tip: if you cannot choose your slot because it has been imposed upon you, and it is the last one, then (to quote Bob) 'cut the crap'. In short, if you know because you are last or – worse – in the yawn-evoking 'graveyard' slot after lunch, and your long-suffering prospect has heard it all before, then cut your pitch to the bare essentials.

ASIDE

Talking of the 'graveyard slot' – that unfortunate time after lunch which causes humans to gasp like fish for fresh air – reminds me of an embarrassing incident. Once, when giving a talk to some one hundred PR people, I spotted one rather glamourous girl in my audience *constantly* yawning. So I mischievously picked on her. I said: 'Do you want to go to bed or something?' There was a faint giggle and a murmur in my otherwise attentive audience.

The next week it was me who was embarrassed, when I read in *PR Week*, our trade magazine, a diary story sent to them by the conference organiser. It (jokingly) accused me of making sexual advances to a delegate. I had received my cumuppance!

Better still if you come last, say: 'You've given us an hour today, but all we need is 40 minutes.' Saving them from further boredom and shortening the time before they can slide off to the pub for a post-pitch bevvy, will endear you to them. But don't go over the 40 minutes you promised (unless it is they themselves that want to lengthen it).

TOP TIP NUMBER 12
USING THE LATEST TECHNOLOGY

No book such as this would be complete without touching on the fantastic opportunities now available for using the latest technology to stage-manage a pitch.

Even though the most inattentive reader will have sussed that I'm a technological dunderhead (it took me the first 25 years of my life to master the use of the lightswitch) I must admit that there is some wonderful kit around these days.

What follows is an idiot's outline guide to what is available.

■ Flip chart – techno version

Technological flip chart you ask? Yes, the simplest of all systems has now been partnered with a photocopier so it will print out in hard copy form what has been written on the chart. OK, its use is not so much for pitches but it's ideal for small think-tank meetings where employees are too lazy to summarise themselves what was put up on the large chart. Of doubtful overall value though, depending on how quickly – like all technology – costs plummet to purchasable levels.

MULTI-MEDIA

From the ridiculous to the sublime. Basically, this system will bring together all the elements you will ever need so that the presenter can show text, graphics, audio and even video all on the screen of a colour portable computer.

As this is ideally viewable by up to six prospects presenters – which must be the optimum in any new business pitch – it has to be where the future lies, provided again that the cost comes down, and the system is idiot-friendly (ie I can use it).

PC DIRECT TO SCREEN

Software which is now available makes for a system that allows what is viewable on a PC screen – the content of your pitch – to be thrown up on to a larger wall-screen. Clearly ideal for larger numbers of people, or members of the partially-sighted prospective clients' association. (Joke.)

LCD 'TABLET' SCREEN

My favourite – because it combines modern technology with one of the most often-used and most adaptable pieces of pitch kit ever: the dear old overhead projector (OHP).

What does its reincarnation in this form achieve? An LCD screen is about one foot square and sits on the OHP. When connected to a PC screen the LCD screen will again enlarge the info up to six feet across. The latest gizmo will even allow the 3D image of a solid object to hit your wall-screen, consigning ordinary typed text to the low-tech dustbin of history (although I'll still use it . . .).

PORTABLE VIDEO

Previously cumbersome, to say the least, video is now pretty portable for pitches held in even the most remote parts of Surrey or Yorkshire. One Japanese manufacturer now sells a system that, using an LCD screen, folds down into a case not much bigger than a shoe-box.

BUSINESS TV

Although costs have now fallen, using TV to hold pitches with prospects some distance away is not yet likely to be an everyday occurance. But it might appeal if you work in a multinational, flush with cash, where floating an idea to colleagues two hundred miles away for an immediate reaction is of value. Certainly, it'll save you the time and money of travel and accommodation – and savings of these two little ingredients (time and money) are a sure-fire method for winning a competitive advantage. So, it's all down to that cost/benefit ratio: if you can make it repay its capital cost pretty quickly, go for it.

Who knows what'll come next: thought transference from your brain to theirs? I hope not.

So much for the physical prompts. But at the end of the day, even an entire car park of prompt slides, portable computers, LCD screens, charts or OHP acetates will only be as good, or as useless, as those people that bring them alive. Just like Sooty, you will be a pretty limp-wristed puppet without Harry Corbett's fist to animate you, if you appreciate the analogy.

And who will bring the puppet show alive? You will. And just how you do that and what you say is what we examine next, in Part Two of Top Tips for the Pitch.

8 TOP TIPS FOR THE PITCH PART TWO: STAND AND DELIVER

PITCH CONTENT: WHAT YOU SAY AND HOW YOU SAY IT

You've straightened out your structure. Your physical supports – audio and visual – are all in place. You've perfected your prompts. So what do you have left to do? You simply have to stand and deliver! But how do you do it? Here are some pointers about what *attitude* to adopt, and on what you say and how to say it, as we continue with part two of our Top Tips For The Pitch.

TOP TIP **NUMBER 13**
FOLLOW THE CHEFKIM FORMULA!

This is by far the most important top tip, and I should know – I invented it. But what does it do? I'll tell you: it encapsulates all the elements that I believe are necessary – even vital – in conducting *any* successful pitch.

Here's what CHEFKIM means:

    C   conviction
    H   humour
    E   enthusiasm
    F   fluidity
    K   knowledge
    I   integrity
    M   modesty

If – through practice – you can keep all these elements at the top of your mind – and eventually use them as a mental guideline for conducting your pitches, then I'll congratulate you, and you can take next Sunday off.

Please keep the CHEFKIM formula pinned to your secretary's chest so that you can always refer to it, no matter which type of pitch, which gender your secretary, or which type of pitch environment you're involved with at any given time.

Think about it. If you can pitch *knowledgeably* (knowing your stuff), with *conviction* (you genuinely mean what you say), *enthusiasm* (it can be catching) and *integrity* (tell them the facts, even if it hurts) – with a British dash of *humour* and *modesty* to go into the cocktail – then you've got yourself a winning formula, I believe. And, of course, the whole event must be linked in a sequential, cogent manner – *fluidity*.

Speaking of being fluid in a pitch, brings me neatly on to – no, not a gin and tonic – but on to the who, what and why sequence that is as fundamental to a pitch as are braces in holding up a pair of trousers. That'll be my next Top Tip.

 TOP TIP NUMBER 14
THE WHO, WHAT AND WHY?

What follows is a microcosm of what you need to read elsewhere,* but it's nevertheless a handy guide to what may seem to state the obvious but which is often overlooked.

WHO?

Remember always to articulate to whom you are pitching. Who are you talking to exactly? What is their competitive status in their industry? Do they currently use one of your competitors? What went wrong with that relationship, assuming something has? Moreover, what is their existing awareness of you? And so on.

WHAT?

Fundamental, but what is your message? Is it a real benefit to them? What is the benefit exactly? How does that benefit relate to what they need or what you already know of them?

* Refer also to the When, Who, Where and Why section in Chapter 1, and to Top Tip Number 20, 'Tap into your audience's interest in themselves'.

WHY?

What are your overall objectives? What response do you want from them? Are you giving them something to buy – something to say 'yes' to?

TOP TIP | **NUMBER 15**
ABOUT KISS, CONCEPT, AND ESCHEWING DETAIL

Remember too, the oft-quoted KISS formula: Keep It Simple, Stupid. It's vital to keep the format *simple* – and this normally means short as well.

As we discussed in Top Tips 1 and 3, learn to think in headlines, in order to get your point across. Don't get bogged down in detail. Why? Because once your audience has got the overall gist of what you're saying, the actual nitty-gritty of how such a strategy can be implemented in tactical terms is *detail*. Your job is to excite them with the concept, not bore them with interminable minutiae. Once they're hooked on the theory, I believe the detail is a matter for another meeting.

In my experience, it's only pedants who will concentrate on the minutiae: the real decision-makers will be those that see the wider picture and those that will buy a strategy in its conceptual form – at least until such time as it might later be proved impractical.

Margaret Thatcher is a good example of someone who often talked in a conceptual manner – or in 'sound-bites', as the media also knows it. Remember 'The lady's not for turning' and the 'Not by the back Delors?' quips? Or what about President George Bush's ominous quip 'Read my lips', and Enoch Powell's controversial 'Rivers of blood' speech? They were all graphic, simple – and thus memorable.

ASIDE

There are plenty of pedants, sadly. There will always be the smart-arse client who, obsessed with detail and unable to see that wider picture, will try and trip you up with questions on specifics. These are dangerous people, because if not handled firmly they will wreck the spirit and drama of your pitch – for everyone. They do it to appear clever in front of their peers – but I believe most are prats. I hate their guts, but I have no strong feelings about the matter other than that.

More to the point, how should one deal with them? The answer is, to comment politely but firmly that the detailed point they are fuming about is covered in a separate document.

Or, you can say that one of your colleagues, who went into such great detail last week to ensure that your proposals will in fact work in practice, will be delighted to convene a separate meeting to allay any fears he may have. In the mean time, because you only have the short timescale of one and a half hours, would he mind ever so kindly not interrupting, and paying attention?

NUMBER 16

HOW TO KEEP YOUR AUDIENCE AWAKE! (BY PROVIDING LIGHT AND SHADE)

One of the best ways to start a presentation is to adopt the assumption that your pitchees will want to take a nap. Your job is to keep them awake and attentive!

The surest way to encourage delegates or prospects into a snooze-induced torpor is to allow your pitch to become the verbal and visual equivalent of a deranged bumble bee: droning on, and on. What you have to provide is contrast, light and shade. Here are three ways to achieve this.

CHANGE AUDIO-VISUAL TECHNIQUES

. . . as you develop the pitch. For example, start the milestones on board; take them through your research on OHP acetate; give them your proposals on slide or personal computer; and perhaps end with your credentials – or some visual back-up to what you've said on video.

You don't have to use all these different techniques, and it doesn't have to be that way round, of course: but the point is that by changing your technique you'll keep them busy and thus deny them their sleep.

CHANGE PRESENTERS

The best idea is to change presenters at the same time as you change certain audio-visual techniques. Make people move around. There's a new voice, a new personality – light and shade – that will keep their attention.

One word of warning, however: don't do it too much, or they'll become giddy or nauseous trying to keep pace as you buzz around like crazed hornets.

USE YOUR VOICE

Above all, use the presenters' voices to provide that light and shade, by giving intonation from time to time: highlighting words or phrases where appropriate. A flat, continuous dialogue is to be avoided at all costs.

NOTE: See also Chapter 6 on 'adrenalin and my confidence shield' and Top Tip Number 18 on adopting the 'stretch mark'.

TOP TIP NUMBER 17

DON'T SET YOUR MIND ON COLLISION COURSE WITH MOUTH (BY ACTING LIKE AN ACTOR)

As I've argued previously, one can effectively render a pitch useless by expecting an audience's mind and eyes to do too much in assessing and understanding a conflicting range of visual and verbal signals – so too, can the speed of delivery screw up the proceedings.

I always think about this when driving through France, down the Bordeaux Autoroute towards my house. Suddenly there is a series of arrows, marked on the road, at various distances apart. Their purpose? To provide a graphic illustration to drivers about their own speed in relation to the driver in front. Now, I adore the French, but driving too close is a national pastime and is certainly not one of their most endearing qualities. (It's bloody dangerous, actually. And annoying.)

And so too, it is with you as a pitcher, if you insist on burbling at

Olympic skier speed through your pitch. OK, I know you're nervous (so try and use my confidence shield, why don't you?). And I appreciate that you are desperate to get to the end of the pitch, with an intensity matched only by the need to empty your bladder following the consumption of 28 pints of Courage Best Bitter, a magnum of Mateus Rosé, or a case of Pimms No 1.

That's no way to proceed – especially if you want people to understand you. But don't worry, it can be cured. How?
Here's how:

1. By stopping your burble.
2. By not starting again . . .
3. . . . until you record yourself on audio cassette, or better still on video so that you can hear and see yourself as others hear and see you.

Above all, you need to pinch yourself, to ensure you pause long enough to allow your audience time to assimilate what you've said. You can't do that if your mind is on a collision course with your mouth. You need to pause, so that the communication (ie the meaning) can be digested, and thus understood.

So remember:

■ speech then
■ silence means
■ communication and
■ understanding.

I'm often asked if we learn from actors. Yes and no is the answer: *yes*, by appreciating how they learn to communicate their words by considered expression; *no*, in the sense that we shouldn't appear in any way false.

Not that the best actors appear false, because with luck we (the audience) will be immersed in the mood they've set for us. But they do learn their lines, after all, and we rehearse our pitch, don't we, so there are real similarities to compare.

The difference between us and actors lies in the fact that we *expect* actors to be doing just that, acting – but no one expects pitchers to be reading or reciting other people's lines, even though this might be the reality, and, like actors, we need to set the mood. We need to learn how to give that 'light and shade' to our rendition, by modulating our delivery. And we need to learn how to pause, and to emphasise certain words and phrases.

We need, in short, to adopt acting techniques – to the extent that we play with our words, rolling them around our mouth slowly until they are released and enunciated clearly. And we are doing this solely to enhance our audience's understanding – no more, no less.

But, by acting, we mustn't become something that we are not:

■ 'Acting' is an advantage only if it enhances our *existing* personality.
■ 'Acting' is a disadvantage if we endeavour to become somebody we are clearly *not* (in reality this will never work, as Top Tip Nmber 19 illustrates). The Top Tip that follows gives a further clue to what I mean.

TOP TIP NUMBER 18
LEARN TO ADOPT THE S T R E T C H MARK

One sure way I've found to give the delivery of a pitch 'space' and a touch of drama is to learn what I call the art of word-stretch. What's that? It's simply elongating key link words in order to accentuate them. Let me give you an example or two. Try it in front of a mirror.

■ A prospect tells you he cannot agree to what you say in your proposal. You retort: 'Maybe not: h o w e v e r, what you c o u l d do is the following . . .'; *or* 'I k n o w what you mean, but you have a c t u a l l y m i s u n d e r s t o o d, if I may s a y so . . . .'
■ A prospect claims black is white. You say: 'Not n e c e s s a r i l y' . . .', before continuing to put him right.

Link this sort of stretch to the 'What can you do . . ./I'll tell you what' in Chapter 6, and the skywards finger pointing, and you're *en route* to a persuasive performance. You'll find your new prospects will stop and look and listen to you if you begin to adopt the 'stretch mark'.

What this also serves to convey is an impression of thoughtfulness and consideration on your part. You are not spitting out words with venomous disregard, but making a kindly point which, because of your languid pace, will be clearly appreciated and understood.

TOP TIP NUMBER 19
DON'T SPEAK LIKE A COPPER

Have you ever listened on radio or TV to a poor old cop describing a crime? It goes something like this:

'A person or persons unknown were seen to illegally enter a parked vehicle when we apprehended them and discovered arms and certain substances about their persons.'

What they meant, of course, was that they niftily nabbed a couple of fellas about to nick a car and found they had guns and pot on them.

But they used their own special language – a certain gobbledegook, hiding behind 'police speak' rather than using real words, in everyday usage, like you and me.

And the moral? It's this: you don't have to invent your own new words when you make an appearance in the board room or in the ballroom, auditorium or studio. Just be yourself – talk and act like you do normally.

JOINING THE CLUB

Conventional wisdom argues that in 'being yourself' you should avoid jargon at all costs. I disagree. I say you *can* – but only if it's clearly explained and made relevant.

My experience suggests that pitchees actually like gaining entry to that 'special club' characterised by industry-speak. It makes them feel special, and this can only be a force for good. But where it works against you is when you use the language without explaining it. By banning pitchees selfishly and stupidly from your special club, in other words.

But I do understand why such codes or languages exist – we all like to wear a special 'uniform' in life (see also 'physical codes', in Chapter 6) that marks us out from the crowd and underlines our exclusive membership of a special tribe, caste or club. It's human nature.

Have you noticed the sudden ubiquitous mentions on consumer TV programmes of the word 'market'? The *Top Gear* motoring pro-gramme on BBC TV talks glibly about the hot hatchback *market*. The *Food and Drink* TV programme, also on BBC, mentions the bottom end of the 'wine *market*'. Such market-share jargon wouldn't have hit the airwaves even just a few years back, being viewed instead as 'industry speak'. But nowadays people understand the meaning, so it's entered common usage.

I have my own language club. If you study the way this book is written, you'll notice I nearly always say 'it's' as opposed to 'it is'. That's (not that is) simply because it's the way I talk: I write like I talk. It's my particular style. Purists for our English language may sniff at it, but that's the way I like it. Years ago, those purists I mention used to criticise me for what they considered slapdash writing. They complained about split infinitives and bad grammar. They were probably right – but my riposte to them was: 'I'm not an academic, I'm a communicator.'

And so too, you must remain at your most natural when you write, speak or pitch. Don't suddenly try to be posh, or 'articulate': if you're not, be yourself – which, paradoxically means that if you *do* normally talk like a policeman, you should continue to do so! (Somehow, however, I can't imagine a policeman at home with his wife talking about apprehending his cat, or proceeding with the vehicle down to the supermarket – can you?)

And that's the nub of it: I don't condone bad grammar, accents or a policeman's delivery *per se*, but I *do* say that the most important consideration is not 'author-correctness' (a subdivision of political correctness?) – but the ability to get one's message across so that your audience understands it.

I'm sure that when policemen use English words, like vehicle, they are totally correct. But do they communicate as well as they could? I think not – and I'll wager that when they are with their mates in the police canteen they speak like you or I. In short, they only become stilted when officialdom paralyses them on the beat or on the TV screen. Make sure you don't fall into the same trap, whatever business yours is.

The conflict between articulation and communication was brought home to me forcibly after a radio interview I once did. I was talking on PR, and the interviewer gave me a lively bunch of questions. In short, he was a trifle aggressive. I thought I did quite well, using humour and anecdotes to puncture his resolve to unseat me.

But when I received a written transcript from a monitoring company, I was appalled! There seemingly wasn't a single finished sentence. There were lots of 'wells' and 'ers' and 'ums'.

I was depressed. What a cock-up! And then, that evening, my wife said she had recorded it onto tape. I recoiled, but soon, after a glass of claret got the better of me, I played it back. My reaction this time? It was brilliant! (Well, half brilliant.)

Why the difference? On air, my 'arguments' came over as being sequential, and (I was relieved to hear) my style perky and fairly convincing. Most importantly, it sounded *natural*.

The moral? Simply, that as a written exercise (ie by reading the written transcript) it seemed to be a flop. But as a verbal communicator? Much better. Not totally articulate or unfalteringly grammatical, but hopefully a communicated message that left its mark.

TOP TIP

NUMBER 20

TAP INTO YOUR AUDIENCE'S INTEREST IN THEMSELVES

Let's be totally honest here. People love themselves to distraction. Whatever is said to the contrary, the fact is most of us have had a romantic affair with ourselves for years (and that includes falling out on occasions, as well). That said, doesn't it make sound business (and social) sense to tap into this resource by enlivening our audience's love affair with themselves?

When we once asked a series of headhunters to pitch to us (we were looking for a non-executive director) the one fault that struck us was that we got no warmth from them. They hadn't clocked that as human beings we might have responded positively to a bit of simple flattery about our successes in building up QBO.

It's always a good idea, therefore, especially before a speaking engagement, to ask the simple questions:

■ Who exactly are the audience?
■ What type of people are they?
■ How can I build a bridge between me and them?
■ How can I flatter their obvious successes?

It matters. You have to make sure who they are. To take an extreme example – you don't recall a sexy story if you're speaking to a clutch of nuns. But more: if you know you will be talking to civil engineers – then you can, if you're clever – twist a story to make it applicable to them.

This can be easier than you sometimes think. I once told such an audience who wanted to run a campaign without research to back up the assumptions they'd made thus:

'You wouldn't build a bridge without first securing the foundations, would you?'

But in a pitch, the pitchees will secretly love to be flattered – provided you don't over-sugar it. So compliment them on their sales record, their reputation, the way their receptionist handled them, or even on the design of their open-plan office. People will only like you for it.*

* See also Chapter 4 on 'You', not 'Me'.

TOP TIP
NUMBER 21
MAY I CALL YOU DARREN?

Never presume that you have permission to use your prospect's Christian name on first acquaintance. Feigning easy familiarity is a mortal sin – especially in the UK. (It's just as bad, incidentally, to write in that way to a complete stranger – those letters to me addressed 'Dear Quentin', from people I don't know, go straight into the bin in my house, for their impertinence.)

But is this just another example of British stuffiness, for which we are reputedly so renowned? No – it's simply common courtesy and common sense rolled into one. Why? Because a prospect knows he is important to you, and a clever pitcher will not destroy the respect that that importance demands.

But you can win his admiration and use his name in a simple manoeuvre: ask permission to call him or her by their first name. Few, if any, will refuse. I always say 'Do you mind if I call you Darren?' (unless he or she is called John or Emma, of course . . .).

I once received a letter about sponsorship from a connection of the Royal Family. It came out of the blue, but I warmed to its contents, which began: 'Forgive me writing to you without an introduction, but . . .'. Stuffiness? No, clever use of old-world charm.

By being polite you will also impress people with your courtesy and help to break the ice. (See also the 'Question' section of the confidence shield in Chapter 6.)

But a word of warning: judge each situation on its merits. Do not risk such a question if your pitchee has clearly had a bad morning already, just been stung by a wasp and had his left foot run over by an ambulance exiting from the out-patients ward, *en route* to the pitch – to take a random example.

It's best he remains undisturbed by matters of a personal nature until he's had several coffees and the pain subsides. And remember – get the Christian name right, in order not to shoot yourself in the foot, as well.

TOP TIP
NUMBER 22
DON'T BE DETERRED FROM REPETITION

I knew a girl once. She was a highly intelligent and articulate broadcaster – a natural. Not that she did it full-time – she was PR spokesperson for her company. But she had one problem – apart from having me as an acquaintance.

She wanted to be *too* good, *too* clever. So, she would always try in radio interviews to present the same issue in a different way on each different programme. It became a challenge *not* to use the same phraseology in – say – six different radio station interviews, even though they were all about the same subject.

Well, each to their own and all that. But I think it was a failing rather than a strength. I believe that once you are into the swing of an interview format and are happy with the level of communication (ie you're saying what you want to say), you should repeat it in each interview. Not word for word, but certainly you can re-use the same arguments, stories, anecdotes and phrases. Why ever not?

I guess people are afraid of being 'caught out', being heard saying the same thing on two stations. But there are so many media opportunities these days, thanks to the many new independent and BBC local radio and TV stations – each with a number of likely specialist programmes that could be interested in your interview. And that is not to mention the emergence of cable and satellite broadcasting – and, of course, the thousands of press magazine columns waiting for your news item or article.

So I say: don't be a hero. Do repeat yourself and your message, even if you are featured on Radio 4's *Today* programme in the morning, the *John Dunn Show* on Radio 2 in the evening, and 14 local radio stations in between. It's highly unlikely that you'll get the same audience of listeners on each show – and for those that do happen to hear you more than once, it may increase their chances of actually understanding you.

If you like to listen to the chat-type programmes that are broadcast on regional stations all over the UK, such as Greater London Radio (GLR) and London Broadcasting (LBC) in the South East, or the BBC nationwide, you'll soon hear the same old celebrities doing the rounds.

I've done just that, leaping from one taxi to another to meet the schedule of appointments. I said roughly the same thing each time – but the raw material (eg launch of a new venture, film, or in my case a new book) was soon embellished with a new view or sprightly anecdote. You can do the same, depending upon your imagination and the interviewer's slant of questions.

So, if you go on the circuit as an industry boss defending your redundancy programme, explaining the drop in your share price, or launching your brand-new gizmo, don't worry. Repeat your key points. Don't be like my girlfriend.

TOP	NUMBER 23
TIP	END WITH A CALL TO ACTION

How do you end a pitch? The first tip is to finish, as previously described, with a succinct reiteration of the key elements of what you've been hurling at them for the last 60 minutes. (See Top Tip Number 3 on 'milestones'.)

But there is a world of difference between that and what I call a positive 'call to action'. This provides them with 'something to buy'.

Remember, even an after-dinner speech should have a purpose: you are rarely speaking just for the hell of it – unless you're famous enough to demand several thousands of pounds simply to be there and elucidate. But few of us are that famous – so always have in the forefront of your mind the purpose of your talk and how you will end (no matter how subtly) with that call to action. Let me give you some examples.

AFTER-DINNER/LUNCH SPEECH

This is an example that may seem initially to be bizarre. It concerns the Foyles luncheons, organised by the wonderful Christina Foyle of the bookshop fame and held at the Grosvenor House Hotel. I have been attending these affairs for years and take a regular table for selected clients. It's a sort of PR 'client-bonding' affair for us. But its purpose for Foyles and for the author of a new book is also undeniably clear, despite the event's genteel air: the guest of honour at the top table at which many other celebrities are seated is there to promote and sell a book. And there's nothing wrong with that – in fact, it's a tradition at the end of the lunch for the author to autograph copies that can be purchased there and then, such is the dynamic 'call to action'.

In fact, it's one of those happy occasions when everybody is happy. The author is selling books. Miss Foyle is promoting her illustrious bookshop (as if she needs to...) My guests are pleased to be in the company of celebrities and on the receiving end of witty speeches. And my company (QBO) has become the catalyst to make it all happen.

I now have signed books by a whole range of actors, broadcasters and politicians on my bookshelf that otherwise wouldn't be there –

varying from Alan Whicker and Michael Parkinson to Nicholas Ridley.

TV/RADIO INTERVIEW

Most of us tend to be led by the interviewer's questions. This is not unnatural, of course, but it can be bad practice. Why? Because you simply play into their hands. They are writing the agenda. You are the victim, they are the masters.

But, with resolve, it can be a simple matter for you to end with a call to action and thus get your point across by concluding in the most apposite manner possible. How can it be achieved? By countering or even ignoring the final question/s, and instead *making your own statement*.

So, for instance when an interviewer is giving you a bad time after the announcement of some staff lay-offs, say:

> No, what I am saying is simply that unless we make these 100 employees redundant, regrettable though it is, we would be forced to close the entire plant, and that would put the jobs of 1000 on the line. This is sad action to face, but what we are achieving is the saving of 900 jobs. That's quite an achievement, in our view.

Or (when an interviewer is trying to trip you up on policy), say:

> Hang-on – let me be quite clear on what I'm saying. I'm saying that the local council must give us permission to extend the factory within the next few days, otherwise we will be forced to lose a substantial contract that will instead give work to thousands of our competitors in Germany.

In both these cases you've made an undeniable call to action, in the sense that nobody can be in any doubt about your views.

NEW BUSINESS PITCH

You've just finished a pitch to 'sell' a marketing programme which you maintain could increase your prospect's profits. How do you conclude? Firstly, you could try the modest approach: 'I hope you find our proposal of interest.'

Secondly, you could adopt a more authoritative tone: 'We very much hope we can work with you on this project.'

Thirdly, you could actually grasp the nettle, as I have on numerous occasions, and ask them a cheeky, direct question: 'What do you think of us [or it]?'

Not everyone would feel cosy about hurling such direct questions across the floor, not least because it may produce an unpleasant surprise: 'Not much, since you ask. I can't see how it'd work in practice.' Ah well, at least in that circumstance you'd know where you stood!

In practice, however, very few pitchees will give you an honest, let alone a rude answer. Not that they're deliberately lying: it's simply that they don't yet know the answer. They need time to mull it over. To pull it to pieces. To be negative about it. That's what management is all about, isn't it – finding out the flaws? (No it isn't.)

In my experience, even the most fantastic proposal, excitedly pitched, will rarely engender an immediate cry of 'You're hired.' Why? Because human nature is such that no one will want to let potential suppliers think right away that they are a gift from God. That would make them far too big-headed – and 'We have our future relationship to consider, after all . . .'.

A QUESTION OF TIMESCALE

Asking a question is the key, except that it shouldn't be one that firmly commits the client to a decision, as that would put their backs up. It should be one that simply commits them to a timescale in which they will make such a decision. That way, you've forced them on the record, to call you 'within the week' or 'next fortnight'.

It's often a glib, off-the-cuff sentiment, but it gives you your justification to contact them again at the prescribed time when they've gone. It's like having a fish on the line. It's hooked, after your pitch, but you're damned if you can bring the slippery chappie into your net at the banks edge. How do you achieve that? That is just one of the aspects we consider in Chapter 9.

9 AFTER THE PITCH – WHAT ACTION NEXT?

In which we learn about post-pitch panic; how to cope with glad or glum tidings; how to use the secretary to reach the heart of Mr Right; why you should ask where you went wrong; and generally how to go about lifting off the artificial cloak of the pitch.

It can be a lonely feeling. One of despair, even. There you are, sitting again behind your old familiar office desk, ruminating on pitches past. Not least of course, the latest one.

As you cogitate, it becomes blindingly clear that only one of three scenarios are now possible.

YOU'VE GOT IT!

The first is that you will soon get a jubilent telephone call, bearing glad tidings. Yippee!

YOU'VE BLOWN IT!

The second is that you get a letter bearing glum tidings. You feel slightly saddened that they feel obliged to hide behind a written missive, rather than being courageous enough to confront you on the blower. But then you remember they too are only human.

Their letter contains all the usual clichés – what a difficult decision it was to make; what a closely-run contest; how truly professional you were, only to come second. *Second*. What an insult! Surely it's better either to win, or – because of your somewhat radical solutions to their problems – to come *last*. But an also-ran? No ta!

YOU DON'T KNOW!

The third scenario is sadly the most commonplace. You hear nothing. Not a dicky-bird. And that's despite their promises. Let's examine how you should handle that situation.

It's three weeks now since the event itself. And by goodness you gave your 'all', leaving the pitch room with your Georgio Armani, Chanel or Marks and Spencer suit looking like a damp rag that'd soaked up all your perspiration.

When you returned to your office your colleagues accosted you with that traditional but damned annoying question: 'How did it go?' You wish you really knew, but the truth is you don't. But you nevertheless retort: 'Seemed to go well . . . I think.'

It's true that they *seemed* to like the pitch. You know because you summoned up your courage and asked them. 'Very good,' they had retorted at the end of the pitch 'you've given us some real food for thought, something to get our teeth into.'

And in answer to your final question about the timescale of their decision-making process, they had said:

'The ball is in our court now. It's up to us to go away and consider what you've put before us. We'll come back next week – in a fortnight at the outside – with our decision.'

So you waited. But after one week you couldn't resist picking up the phone. At first you held back. You didn't want to appear too keen: this might give the impression that you desperately need their business in order to shore up that cavernous hole in your cash flow. Better to be slightly arrogant, you reason – stand-offish even. Better to give them the impression that there are so many other clients knocking at your door that you simply don't need the Acme metal company's business anyway. Let them come to you, that's the best way to sell.

But then your resolve weakens. You've looked again at that cash-flow forecast . . . . You called them. 'I'm afraid Mr Right is in a meeting at present,' came the ominous reply – made even more so the more often the same thing happened. *Always* in meetings? Surely not.

You discussed the dilemma with your colleagues. It could mean one of four things:

1. He *is* in meetings. A busy bloke, Mr Right there's no doubt.
2. He is avoiding us – but this needn't be bad news. Maybe he hasn't had time to convene a debriefing meeting in order to make a decision, but that decision – when made – is just as likely to be in our favour as any of our competitors.
3. He is avoiding us (the bummer) because his firm is about to hire one of our competitors – and he's too yellow-bellied to ring us with the bad news.
4. Worse still, he's avoiding us because he's decided to hire nobody and to try instead to undertake the project himself with an internal

team internally, pinching our ideas for their own (unethical) benefit.

Ah well! To those reading this tome who have already been in the role of pitcher, that sad scenario of avoidance will be all too familiar.

Getting the little darlings to make up their mind can be worse than trying to score goals in a cricket match. And one thing is beyond any doubt – if they won't answer your calls there is little you can do about it, short of bursting into their offices with a contract in your clammy fist and a meat cleaver in the other.

But the truth is there are many natural barriers that often cause this problem. Like internal client politics, where their chairman – who wasn't even at the pitch – is against the consensus because his wife wants to hire the local firm, for example.

Or there's a disagreement about which supplier to hire, because of a post-pitch change of strategy amongst those who attended the event: it was the pitch process itself that convinced them their original thinking was wrong, and thus now the goalposts are changed.

You go over everything in our own mind. You're convinced you did everything right:

- It was a good pitch – content and execution.
- Your price was competitive.
- You enjoy a good market reputation in your industry, and they had a high regard of you.
- You asked the prospect at the conclusion of your pitch the following:
  — what steps did he intend to take from now?
  — was he going to see any of your competitors?
  — How many, and whom?
  — How long was it going to be before a decision?

So, what more, you ask yourself, can you reasonably do? Not much, on the face of it, I agree. But you must.

Because if your pitchee won't pick up the phone or respond to your letters you have a real problem – but what you *must* do nevertheless is keep up the dialogue. Just as I argued in Chapter 3, when I described the new business wheel, you're in this for the long-term, not for a quick fix.

And I can't believe that many prospects will continue to be so doggedly uncommunicative: your consistency of follow-up will make them feel hellishly guilty in the end. So keep up the dialogue. Keep up the pressure. Write and phone regularly to follow it up at reasonably spaced intervals – every ten days or so, for example. And remember, if it gets really bad, you can be inventive. Here's some ideas:

- Get an old-fashioned style of telegram made up measuring 2 feet by 1 foot by an art studio with a message begging that they indulge you with a reply. Have it delivered by an actor dressed as a pageboy . . . and have the handover to their receptionist photographed, with the pic sent in afterwards to all those pitchees, plus their Chairman.

- Buy a single poster sight, conveniently situated by the road outside the prospects' office window and get an ad agency to work up a special message for him. Make it amusing but pertinent. This can then also be photographed, but this time sent to the pitchee's industry's trade magazine as a news story – just in case he should miss the original poster. (Well, if your potential contract is valuable this expensive method could work – and it's been tried before . . . .)

- Get your PR firm to mock up an editorial story in the same typeface and style of either his trade press or a national newspaper, stating that 'Company X has succeeded in increasing its profits following the appointment last year of [your company].' In short, provide a spurious, hypothetical, retrospective article to demonstrate how successful your service has been and thus will be.

- Get an old-fashioned bakelite telephone (or a Micky Mouse one?) and package it in a box with the message 'This phone must be used to telephone [your name] of [your firm] in order to finalise contract/ get campaign going, etc etc.' Don't be tempted, however, to say 'This phone was built 30 years ago. Will it take you that long to phone me?'

- Get a beautiful young lady, or a reproduction Chippendale (of the muscular male variety) to deliver a six-foot tall cardboard cut-out of you with a speech bubble coming from your mouth saying: 'It'll only take three minutes of your valuable time to give me an update of the current position regarding our pitch.'

- Or, alternatively, the same messengers could deliver a six-foot cut-out of the pitchee, saying something similar or even with him mouthing: 'I'm glad to say (your firm) has been awarded the contract.'

Now, some of the above may seem far-fetched to you. And indeed, there is a danger that some recipient-prospects will, like Queen Victoria, be 'not amused'. But it can be a risk worth taking if you feel you've made a relevant and good pitch; if you really want that contract because you know the job is right up your alley; if it's potentially worth a lot of money to you; and if no other method will induce your prospect to contact you.

My feeling is that not many prospects are hard-nosed enough to overlook your inventiveness, and more to the point, your sheer

If they don't answer your calls there is little you can do about it short of
bursting into their offices.

---

enthusiasm at wanting to win the contract. It should induce them to
contact you – even if it means bad news when they finally do.

But not all prospects suffer from apathy or indecision. Most
genuinely will agree to, or even want to keep up a dialogue – and some
will willingly admit their indecision. In this situation, what can you
then do to further your cause? You basically need to provide your
prospect with the answer to the following question: 'What more
information can I possibly give in order for you to make up your mind
to hire us?'

And the answer to the question? It involves asking him in to see you
working in an everyday situation, outside the unreality of the pitch.
Offer to open up your company to him or her in other words. Invite
the prospect into your office. So, if at the pitch you presented a team
that would work on their business, make them available – but *in situ*.
Put a human face on your humans. Show how your systems will back
them up. Show your people working to solve another client's problem,
and thus demonstrate how it'll work for the prospect. Involve them in

the process – it's not good enough to simply wheel them into a pitch for 90-odd minutes and then wheel them out again after you've been through the 'team hierarchy' bit (see Top Tip number 9, Chapter 7).

You need to put psychology to work. Bring your prospect on your side, at your patch, into your metaphorical bosom as a potential partner.

THEIR WINNING WAYS: ROBERT BEAN, HEAD OF ADVERTISING, BT

'I'm astounded that most people don't do this,' said Bob Bean to me, 'because it seems such an obvious thing to do after a pitch to help clinch the deal,' He was referring to such an offer – the open-door invitation following a pitch in order for the prospect to look over the supplier (in his case, his ad agency) to see 'what it's like to work with us'.

It's a perceptive point – the chance for the prospect to see what life would be like if he were a client – access to how things operate and how all teams work together with a client in solving the prospect's problems.

Why perceptive? Because we all know the pitch situation is somewhat artifical – it has to be by definition: it's ninety minutes of unreality, bearing no resemblance to the working days that will follow. The open invitation dispels the mystique; it provides a 'smell and taste', demonstrating a supplier made up of real people, real experts. In short, it overlays a real-life human face by lifting off the artificial cloak of the pitch.

My guess is that if an offer providing access of this magnitude fails to impress, then you were on a pretty sticky wicket anyway. But in most pitch situations, where there is generally only a narrow line between your own performance and not of your competitors (although not always, if my research in Chapter 10 is to be believed), I'll wager it'll help you win the day.

Why? Because prospects buy people – and you've built a bridge for your guys to meet him and his guys. This bridge is especially welcome in the marketing services business, where any attempt to open up the advertising or PR agency will be a wondrous step forward in demolishing the often rightly perceived arrogance of the professionals who inhabit this world.

But what reaction do you envisage prospects will give to this caper? It can produce different reactions from dear old clients. Some will welcome it, saying: 'If he's taken the trouble to ask me, I'll go. That's a feather in their caps.' Others, however, will be very proper and reserved about such shinanigans, claiming 'We don't want to give an unfair advantage to one supplier over another even after the event, so we'll decline your invitation, thank you very much.'

What attitude would *you* take if you were the prospect? I would go for it: I would persuade myself that I can only learn more and it might give me enough extra emotional or even rational background to help me to make a decision where it is a close race between all the contenders.

But what happens if all else fails to get your Mr Right on the blower? Here's our answer.

GET THE SECRETARY ON YOUR SIDE

It amazes me how many so-called 'salespeople' put secretaries' backs up when, in fact they should be courting them. Why do they do it? One reason I'm sure is that they see the good old sec as a barrier to the boss. In reality, this is quite often the case. But such barriers can often be quickly turned into bridges.

I've lost count of the number of times an aggressive salesperson has slammed down the phone on Beverley Walker, my secretary. The reason? Because he (it's always a 'he') insists on talking to me personally but refuses to give details of who he is before being put through.

I have a simple rule. I'll speak to anyone (within reason) provided they:

1. Explain beforehand who they are, from which company.
2. Explain beforehand briefly what they want.

Of course, many of the more devious callers will have the sole objective of speaking directly to 'the man that matters', in the knowledge that he rarely actually wants to take the call, but once through they'll have the best chance of earholing him in order to sell their wretched photocopiers or life assurance. They'll know too, that if they say they're from Acme Life Assurance at the outset, it's unlikely that they'll be put through. (They'll be right.)

But generally, if someone genuinely feels they have something to say that will interest me, and can provide my secretary with a thumbnail sketch of what it's about (and they are not selling photocopiers or life assurance), I'll take the call. But there must be many genuine callers who fail simply because they fail the 'secretary test'.

So how exactly do you build bridges with a secretary and win the test? Here's how.

GET HER NAME BEFOREHAND

An obvious point, but often overlooked. All you have to say to the switchboard is: 'I'd like to speak to Mr Right's secretary, but I've forgotten her name.' The chances are high you'll get it – because people simply like to help.

DO YOU HAVE A MOMENT?

Always start your conversation gently and politely. The idea is not to get the secretary's hackles up – there are likely to have been many calls that have done that already, and so the secretary may possibly be in defensive mood automatically. So the trick is to be disarming and courteous. And that is achieved by asking if the secretary has the time to actually talk to you. But you must succinctly say who you are first – preferably by referring instantly to a 'common point' between you. This could be the letter you have sent, thanking Mr Right and his team for attending your pitch and inviting him in to see your operation first-hand. Or you could simply preface your remarks and provide that vital link between you thus:

> I'm Darren Dreamcoat from Dreamcoat Services – we met Mr Right last week at our pitch. I was wanting some advice from you. Do you have a moment?

Now that's a magical formula: you did three vital things in the space of a few (but equally vital) opening seconds of the call. They were:

- You provided that psychological link between yourself and Mr Right, to give the secretary signals that you were a 'friend', not a 'foe'. ('We met Mr Right last week at our pitch.')
- You asked for advice – something we all love to give, and love to be asked for even more. ('I would like some advice from you.') Why? Because we all like to help – and to be able, in a sense, to show our 'superiority' by being the owner of information that others want. It's plain human psychology: people just adore giving advice.
- You asked if the secretary had time to speak to you. ('Do you have a moment?'). Right away, this gives signals that, by inference, you value the secretary's time. You realise they are busy, and by implication are an important person in the organisation, not a lackey to be ignored or abused.

Of course, if the secretary is genuinely busy (something which most callers imagine is impossible, arrogantly assuming instead that secretaries have all the time in the world to talk) then you should ask: 'When would be the best time to call you? First thing in the morning, after lunch, or at teatime?' This narrows down the field of operation by providing three opportunities to choose from – rather than by providing a blander, open question.

But getting the secretary on your side won't guarantee that Mr Right will acquiesce with your plans – let alone hire you. However, it will give you the best shot possible at succeeding in what are otherwise difficult circumstances.

ADDRESS HER IN HER OWN RIGHT

Rather than falling into the common trap of using the secretary as a dumb conduit in order to get a message to Mr Right, address *her* as your prospect, not *him*. In other words, speak to her in her own right. Involve her in your problem. Explain your predicament. Say: 'I wonder if you can help me', or 'What do you think is my best way forward?' In short, ask for advice, bring the secretary on your side and make her the subject of your pitch.

PUT IT IN HIS DIARY

If you are intending to invite Mr Right in to see your chaps and chapesses, as previously described – and there's evidently no way you can get through to him personally – get the secretary to put a tentative date in his diary. She's your friend and ally now, remember. So you can suggest that, as custodian of his every movement, she pencils in a time and day when he is free. It just might work. Why? Because this way Mr Right has to actively cancel the appointment – and this requires more positive action than just simply ignoring you. And, of course, it brings you and your enthusiasm to his attention again.

But what about the other scenarios? The one where, particularly, you lost the contest? Do you shoot yourself? No, you do two things.

The first is to telephone – or write first, saying you will then telephone – in order to find out why you lost. It provides vital intelligence and is sadly often overlooked. So be brave. Say how sorry you were to lose – and then ask if he or she wouldn't mind telling you why. Explain that it is simply your intention to learn from your mistakes. And, not only will they be impressed with that sentiment, you will actually risk learning something.

Were your competitors better, or were you just plain bad? Did they come up with better ideas or a better programme? Did the prospect like the other people better? Were you too pushy, or too technical? You'll probably find out – and you can adjust your next performance accordingly; although in reality you'll find that what appeals to one prospect, appals another, so it's best to be faithful to 'what you are'.

In a *Campaign* magazine article on the topic ('The death of the pitch is nigh' by John Tylee, 30 October, 1992), the very same question was popped. Here's what the article said:

> So how do you bounce back after an unsuccessful pitch? First, says Stubbings [John Stubbings, Deputy Managing Director of ad agency Dorlands] you have to be sure the client didn't leave the pitch hating your guts. Second, ask the client what you did wrong. Some, such as Tony Hillyer, the director of brand marketing at Britvic, will identify the good and bad points about the agency's unsuccessful pitch.

So, what else do you do apart from ask that question? The second thing you do is to pop the cork of a bottle of vintage champagne and invite your pitch team to join you, even if it is 8.00 am in the morning. Why? Because you must accept these truths:

■ Accept that you can only do your best – which you did.
■ Accept the inevitable – that even with the best pitch in the world, and the best team in the world to deliver it, you simply will not win them all. It's quite simply beyond your control.

But why champagne? I don't exaggerate in my choice of the particular liquid, became the point I'm making is that there is only one element vital to the success of any business: confidence. And that's what, even in your hour of solemnity, you need to inspire.

The last thing you want from your team is a sea of glum faces. So, give them some bubbly, congratulate them on their effort – and keep their spirits up. Why? Because you've just had a call to invite you to another pitch. And who knows, fortified by that glass of champagne – and brimming with confidence – you'll probably win that one.

At first you held back. But then your resolve weakened – you've looked again at your cash flow forecast. *Had* you won their business?

10 HOW TO KEEP CLIENTS (ONCE YOU'VE WON THEM)

In which we discover the virtues of openness, security and confidence; and how to turn client expectation into reality.

There is no magic wand that, once waved, will ensure that the multi-million pound slice of business you've just won won't spin out of the other side of your lobby's revolving door within a couple of weeks. It can happen. Whilst only one person can tell you how to run your business in terms of the service you offer – and that's you – there are tricks of the trade to learn when it comes to structuring your relationship during those crucial first few weeks of the honeymoon period.

This is a phenomenally challenging time: you've hooked the fish and won the business, but now you have to learn to cajole, caress and pamper your spoils if they are not to break loose before you've safely manoeuvred them to the bank's edge for good. And it's all about inspiring confidence in your client.

Here are some tips to help you guide our metaphorical fish permanently to shore.

ARRANGE AN IMMEDIATE DEBRIEF

One vital lesson to learn is to ensure your catch is not left dangling in a vacuum once you've won the business. There is a danger that you may be either so relieved or so joyous at your success that you will overlook the need to 'pamper' them. Remember, from the client's point of view this is a testing time when their high expectations have to be converted by you into a semblance of reality. They won't expect your programme of activity to be launched immediately at full throttle, of course, but they will expect you to professionally nurture them, to guide them along the new road they've taken.

136

And that's where the debrief comes in. This is the most useful of tactics for the purpose of pampering them. It provides an immediate bridge between your euphoria in winning and their nitty-gritty expectations of working with you in the cold light of day. So, set up a debriefing session, in which every item of your pitch is dissected and discussed. You'll need to know exactly how well your pitch proposals were received, not just for your own idle enjoyment but because you now need to tie things down and start to make things happen. I'm going haywire with my metaphors, but look at it this way: the critics have given you a good first-night review; now you have to get the show on the road.

The debrief has the underlying purpose of also providing a mechanism or platform for the client and supplier to get to know each other in a different environment: no longer are you strangers-of-the-pitch, but partners, working together with the same goals.

I've undertaken several debriefs where it transpired that very little of what we proposed was actually implemented. We won the business because they liked the way we went about things, the style of our pitch and the personality of our people. So when we sat down to go through the pitch document they closed their copy and said: 'Now, let's talk more openly about our situation.' The point I'm making is simply that the debrief provides that vital psychological platform for the relationship to get off on the right foot – for the client to be, perhaps, able to speak more openly with you than before.

DON'T PASS DOWN THE PYRAMID

I've mentioned this point before, in Top Tip number 9, in Chapter 7, but it's so important that it bears repeating. Nothing pisses off a new client more than finding out that the guy whom he was led to believe would be his link-man now has better things to do. So, don't immediately pass all the responsibility to the tea-boy, but make sure the client is totally *au fait* with the different levels of contact within your company, and who does what.

I recommend that all law firms, accountants and the like implement the account-structure favoured by advertising agencies and PR firms. This makes the team format totally transparent: who the account director is (ie the strategic link-man); who the account manager is (ie responsible for day-to-day execution), etc. The client will know where he stands. There'll be no unpleasant surprises. And he is less likely to sack you after the first week.

Let me give you some examples:

■ If you're an accountancy practice, decide who will deal with your client's tax affairs, who will handle the throughput of the monthly management accounts, and who will oversee both as 'account director'. And put this information down in writing, for the client to keep.
■ If you're a law firm, decide who will deal with your client's acquisition work, who will handle litigation, and who will oversee both as 'account director'. And put it down in writing for the client to keep.
■ If you're a design firm, decide who will deal with your client's creative work (and in my view, do let the scruffy creatives talk to your client); who will co-ordinate print activity, and who will oversee both as 'account director'. And put it down in writing for the client to keep.

All this can do is give him confidence – he's dealing with a team of professionals, and that can only be to the good.

CONTACT REPORTS

There is a lot that we can learn here from the marketing services sector. So get yourself some special 'contact report' paper printed, over and above your normal letterheading. And use it to make copious notes of not just every meeting you have, but of telephone calls, too.

What effect will that have? It'll not just protect you from any future misunderstandings or arguments on what was agreed, but it'll present your firm as a professional outfit that is in charge of events. In short, you are a 'safe pair of hands'. And that's what clients want – security – if they're not to leave, unexpectedly and in acrimonious circumstances.

ACTIVITY REVIEWS

One of the biggest dangers in an ongoing relationship is supplier apathy. Everything seems to be going so well that you can relax your standards a bit. But you can't – not if you're clever.

One sure way to keep your internal team on its toes is to instigate monthly, quarterly or half-yearly activity reviews – whichever is most suitable – in addition to the regular meetings that take place as a matter of course. That can really concentrate the mind: how can you stand up in front of your paymasters and count your successes on his behalf if there haven't been any? The best way to keep a client is to ensure your teams know they have to perform and are going to have to justify themselves at the regular reviews. That'll help them make work to projects on schedule!

PLAN OF ACTION

It's no good staging an activity review unless you have a proper internal plan of action, on how to achieve your goals, with timescales attached.

But why not also make this plan available to the client? You may initially think that such a rash action will expose you too much to your client, giving him too many expectations. But why not be brave? An engineering consultant will have a step-by-step plan on how to build that bridge (or whatever), so why not articulate it in front of the client on a specially printed activity plan/timescale? Marketing services firms of any note have, of course, pioneered this technique with media plans, campaign schedules, and so forth.

Certainly headhunters could do the same – itemising now long it will take to source new target personnel, through to offering one a job and seeing them begin. Couldn't it work for you? And why not lawyers, accountants and architects? I don't see any reason why not. But the key is to print up a special form for the purpose (see Figure 14) with your logo on it – and to give it to the client for his information. That way you've shown you're in charge, and that you have the courage of your convictions. You've demonstrated the professionalism of your infrastructure, and given the client confidence that he's in safe hands.

ADMIT YOUR MISTAKES

The thing clients hate most of all is when their supplier tries to cover up a mistake. But it's just as bad when that supplier is not first to draw the client's attention to the rotten deed: the client himself discovers it. What you must always do is 'up-front' any error, immediately. Pick up the phone, and don't delay by deluding yourself that it will 'all go away', or the client 'won't find out'.

We once returned £40,000 of consultancy fee to compensate for a genuine overcharge that, believe it or not, the client hadn't initially noticed. We believe our honesty won us his respect, despite the fact that it drained our bank account of profits we'd assumed were ours. By admitting such a fault, you will at least be in charge of events. The last thing you want is for the client to find out first – then he will be furious

The Quintin Bell Organisation plc

PR PLAN/CALENDAR 1992

CLIENT
PRODUCT

PROJECT	JAN	FEB	MAR	APR	MAY	JUN	JUL	AUG	SEP	OCT	NOV	DEC

Figure 14 Example of a project activity plan/timetable.

both about the mistake and the fact that he discovered it first – making him doubly angry, and putting you on the defensive.

Most mistakes can be smoothed over. There may be the occasional mega-blunder that renders you sacked on the spot, of course, but this is a rare event for the professional outfit. Most blunders can be put down to human error. And the best way to recover is to up-front it to the client immediately, apologise, and give the reason why it happened. They are human, too, remember.

But back to plans and timescales. Some suppliers will baulk at putting such things in writing on forms to clients, because they can then be held to ransom when what was promised doesn't materialise. But this is small-time and short-term thinking – and there is always a reasonable excuse that a reasonable client will accept if it's reasonably put. External forces may have intervened, for example. Or maybe even the client is at fault, for not completing something at his end (be tactful!). But the overriding key is: admit your mistakes, openly and quickly.

TELEPHONE REGULARLY – BUT FOR A REASON

Keep regular contact on the phone, so that you are seen as a 'real' person, and not a distant figure that continually fires off letters, contact reports and faxes. But you must strike the right balance between welcome dialogue and pain-in-the-bum hassler. Let me explain.

I was eating recently in one of my favourite Chinese restaurants when I had to stop the waiter being too attentive to the wine bottle. He hovered around, and after I'd had just one sip he'd aim to fill it up as soon as the glass came to rest on the table. I began to get annoyed. Apart from the prospect of getting pretty drunk, pretty quickly, I thought his idea of perfect service was over the top. So I asked him to leave the bottle for us to dispense at our own relaxed leisure.

Can you guess what happened? Yes – he went from being over-attentive to being over-there! In other words, I couldn't get his attention even for ready money when I wanted to order more dishes. The pendulum had swung from one extreme to the other.

The same is true of your telephone relationship with your client. It's vital you stay in touch, but it's even more vital you don't do it too much by picking up the phone when you feel you *should* talk but you have nothing specific to say. But phoning too little is equally bad. Get the balance right by following up on a real issue, and use the call to cover the minor points – or social chit-chat as well.

BE PLEASANTLY SURPRISING

Keeping to your stated plan is great – but there is nothing better calculated to ensuring that you keep your client than to give him or her an extra pleasant surprise.

The action plan will give them comfort that you are progressing things nicely and on target – but that extra little gem will work wonders. As an example or two:

- Tell the client you recommend that if he puts XYZ investments in an offshore trust he'll save thousands in tax (if you're an accountancy practice).
- Tell the client that you've managed to negotiate an unexpected TV spot during the main film in prime time at half price due to a sudden cancellation (if you're an advertising agency).
- Tell the client you've got his Chairman an unexpected interview on ITN's *News At Ten*, to win some brownie points (if you're a PR firm).

And so on. The pleasant surprise is always something the clients will remember for a long time. And, what's more, it will put something in the 'deposit account' to pull out and set against your blunder when and if you screw up at a later date.

DEMONSTRATE YOUR SUCCESSES

Human nature being what it is, clients will more easily remember the cock-ups than they will the times when the ship is in calm waters with everything going swimmingly. So always adopt a policy of modestly reminding them of your successes, no matter how trivial you may find them because of your own familiarity with them. What comes easily to you, may be mind-blowingly fabulous to them. Don't take your successes for granted, because your client certainly will if you don't remind him from time to time. And, so that it doesn't appear disjointed, always try and keep your main claims to the official activity review. It's better to make a big (albeit modest) play with some drama, than lose the impact via many odd fragmented phone calls.

DO WHAT YOU SAY!

Here we end with the best gem of all. One of the surest ways to part company with your new client is to hear him moan:

The promise of what they'd do and what they'd achieve was
what won them our business. But I'm very disappointed with
the reality . . . they're not living up to it.

And remember, 'living up to it', of course, includes 'doing the
business' as much as it does the manner in which that business is
conducted. In short, you must make sure when you say a project will
be completed that you *do* complete it (or that you've got a good reason
why not); when you say you'll telephone that you *do* telephone – and
so on.

And that brings us full circle: the unreality of the pitch, and all the
drama and all the adrenalin you put in will be to no avail if you cannot
deliver the goods on the day.

What you can do, however, is buy yourself plenty of time by
cuddling your new client with a corporate corset made up of the ten
tips in this chapter. Remember, it's better during the honeymoon
period to appear brilliant but be average, than the other way round!

But what do the clients think themselves? I asked them – and the
answers are in Chapter 11.

JUST ONE MORE THING (OR HANG ON A MINUTE BEFORE WE CLOSE . . .)

11

WHAT DOES THE CLIENT ACTUALLY WANT?

In which we learn a lot about what the client thinks for a change, and discover we've travelled the round trip of the pitch back to the first Fundamental Truths.

We've talked one heck of a lot in this book about how *we* should behave: how we should duck and dive, even cavort in order to present our best side in the pitch. And, by definition, that means we've taken into account a lot about how our target feels. Because no one, after all, can pitch in a vacuum. As I have pleaded in the previous pages, we all have to know, or attempt to know, what our audience – the prospect – wants. But do we really know enough?

Maybe not. Well, if not, then the best way to find out is to ask them. And that's exactly what I did: I decided to undertake some research, ably assisted by McCallum Layton in Leeds – a first class, professional small research firm who've done a lot for QBO and its clients in the past.

What I did was to survey the opinions of some 30 key marketing directors residing in some of the UK's top 'brand' companies. Why marketing directors? Because, quite simply, this group have the most experience of 'being pitched to' – and often by some of the world's most proficient pitchers in the game: the advertising, PR and other marketing services suppliers who are experts at this skill. What's important to remember is that the results will be directly applicable to your business as well.

So what did the research reveal? Well, I'm glad to say that generally speaking their opinions supported wholeheartedly the points I'm expounding in this book. (And yes, I conducted the research after the majority of the book was written.) What follows are the key headline findings to the questions, with my personal assessment attached to each:

Q1 How many potential suppliers are appraised before you select those asked to actually pitch (ie asked to present credentials)?

A1 The majority (62 per cent) favour between six and ten companies, followed by 24 per cent who believe 1–5 companies are sufficient. The average number is 8.

QB'S ASSESSMENT

I'm surprised at this one. Five credentials are the optimum number, but no more. Any more and the prospect will become entirely confused, thereby making his work in choosing an agency more difficult, not easier. The management that chooses up to ten suppliers to vet are trying to be *too* objective, and apart from wasting an enormous amount of unnecessary management time, they will in truth end up with as subjective an assessment as anyone else. What happens in my experience is that sod's law rules and the same assessment team will not be constant in vetting each and every supplier. In other words, some key members will miss some of the meetings because of constraints on their time, rendering the affair a complete and expensive farce. And not a fair one either.

Q2 How many companies are finally selected to pitch?

A2 A massive 90 per cent believe between three and four companies is best. The average number is three.

QB'S ASSESSMENT

I agree that this is a sensible and sane outcome.

Q3 What were the top points that influenced you in choosing these pitchees?

A3 First came their track record/reputation/word of mouth (55 per cent). Second equal (at 31 per cent) were creativity/quality of idea and size/stature of the company. Understanding of product/market/brief weighed in at just 28 per cent.

QB'S ASSESSMENT

That 'reputation' romped home first endorses my original point in Chapter 2 about the power of fame – but I'm frankly surprised that 'understanding our product/our business/our brief' weighed in at a sad fourth, after 'size/stature', which in itself is an interesting one. Why? Because not all companies can be 'big' – but all companies can be and should be astute enough to work proactively at nurturing their reputation. That is in their total control – so go and hire a PR firm!

Q4 What is your preferred location for the pitch?

A4 Client's own premises comes top at 41 per cent, with agency premises a whisker away at 38 per cent.

QB'S ASSESSMENT

A narrow verdict here, thus showing that the factor appears to be of little or no consequence to pitchees. The 41 per cent of clients that favoured their own premises presumably did so on the grounds of saving themselves the trouble of travel, and arguably to make them feel secure on their home ground. But 38 per cent believed it's best to go to the supplier. I take my hat off to these people, because they take the trouble to see the pitcher on his home territory and thus get a fuller and more rounded feel for the corporate culture and pitching environment. They will be the gainers in amassing more relevant information about their potential suppliers than those lazy stop-at-homes.

Q5 How much time do you allocate for the pitch?

A5 The majority (64 per cent) allocated 1.5–2 hours, with 57 per cent setting aside half an hour or less of that for questions. However, as many as 28 per cent didn't allocate a specific time, and a surprising 41 per cent preferred asking questions during the pitch (as opposed to 17 per cent at the end of it and 38 per cent with no preference).

QB'S ASSESSMENT

The one-and-a-half-hour timescale, as suggested in this book, appears to be the norm. But I wonder how many pitches might in reality go over this time without the players realising it? Time flies when you're enjoying yourself, after all. What is interesting, however, is the high proportion of prospects who prefer to interrupt (my word) the pitch flow during the event, rather than waiting to the end. This is a tricky one: ideally it is better to allow pitchers their full 60 minutes – not least because often an interruptive question will be about a topic that is about to be raised anyway in the course of the pitch. By stopping the flow, all the prospect has succeeded in doing is achieving an unnecessary and often annoying disturbance. On the other hand, there are genuine times when a point is misunderstood and needs illumination, in order to move on.

The golden rule is, I believe: yes, interrupt for simple clarification of a point, but not for a major discourse on the 'meaning of life'. (Note: also see Chapter 5, New Business Pitch Timeframe.)

Q6 How long should a credentials pitch last?

A6 The majority (62 per cent) believe it should last between one and ten minutes. However, a substantial 24 per cent think 11–15 minutes is acceptable; and 14 per cent even believe 16–20 minutes is OK.

QB'S ASSESSMENT

It depends on the occasion – and the type of company which is pitching. Sometimes a longer creds is acceptable if a specific case history or two is particularly relevant to the proceedings – this sort of creds can take an hour and still be succinct – and meaningful. In general, however, I feel that any supplier who can't get a creds covering their history, structure and experience in under ten minutes, is a prat.

Q7 Do you think suppliers spend too much time on credentials, and boast too much when doing them?

A7 Interestingly, as many as 69 per cent believe that creds are too long, with only 28 per cent feeling the time to be 'about right'. Equally, an astonishing 66 per cent believe suppliers boast too much, with only a sane, healthy 31 per cent believing this not to be true.

QB'S ASSESSMENT

Not surprisingly, prospects feel suppliers are too full of themselves – and some of the time they're probably right. Generally speaking – though not always – it's best to keep it to ten minutes (see Q6). There's a heck of a lot one can cram into that time, and any extra can become repetitious dross. It's all back to the art of keeping things simple.

But what about the boasting allegation? This comes back, I believe, to the attitude of the pitchers, as mentioned in Chapter 4. There is another aspect to this: some prospects are envious of their suppliers' apparent success, although they'll never admit it, and sour grapes may be coming through here in the figures. Management consultants, advertising and PR firms and headhunters are often still viewed as profligate in their lifestyles – even if this is only partly true.

But, in any event, why should a successful supplier apologise for that success? That's one of the reasons he or she is being *hired* anyway, isn't it? One wouldn't pay fees to a downtrodden fool, would one? But it's equally true that one person demonstrating a success story for another client that is relevant to the particular pitchee's situation can do so modestly, whilst another can seem bumptious. It's simply how it's done that matters.

Q8 How many, on average, present to you at a pitch? What is your ideal, preferred number?

A8 The largest number (31 per cent) are actually subjected to three people, with 28 per cent four people and 24 per cent five people. The average number is 3.9.

The highest number (35 per cent) prefer three people, followed by 31 per cent preferring four people and 17 per cent five or six. The average number preferred is 3.5.

QB'S ASSESSMENT

A mind-boggling and boringly balanced result this: it seems that what is preferred is actually what is received. Is this a world-first, I ask? But it's correct: keep your team to four or under; but don't field .5 of a person for fear of upsetting them!

Q9 What number of people from your side do you – the client – normally have present at a pitch?

A9 Forty-five per cent of client prospects field two or three people, 41 per cent between four and five. Average number is 3.9.

QB'S ASSESSMENT

I'm gob-smacked that clients field an average of 3.9 people, as this is exactly the number who come from the supplier's camp. I've heard about a balanced budget, but this is spooky. (Do you think the .9 people converse with each other?)

Q10   How much does the standard of the content of the pitch vary between suppliers?

A10   A massive 87 per cent believe it does vary, either 'very much' or 'quite a lot'. Of the remainder who didn't believe it varied very much, the majority (75 per cent) said their final selection is based on the 'cost' and 'people' factors (assuming content to be equal in standard).

QB'S ASSESSMENT

This one surprises me greatly – especially as the respondents (marketing directors) are in a business with which I'm accustomed. This is a smallish sample, of course, and some might say that the figures cannot be relied on for complete statistical integrity.

But that apart, I have always believed that most competing firms in the marketing services sector reach a threshold of competence that they share between them. What they would produce at the pitch in terms of content, in other words, is quite similar.

■■■■■■■■■■■■ **FT Number 30** ■■■■■■■■■■■■

It's the personalities that execute it, and their attitudes – plus the reputation of the outfit – that will provide the truly secure discriminator in a win or lose scenario.
■■

But my feelings are clearly not shared by the research sample. Or could there be another explanation? I think there could.

What I think underlies this point is the issue of creative work submitted by advertising agencies, sales promotion or PR firms. It's on this aspect that they've based their answers and this, being viewed subjectively by the prospect, invokes an emotional response each time. It would explain why there appears to be so much of a perceived variance in the standard of pitch content.

Or am I wrong? Are suppliers really different in their pitch approach? Is one headhunter, lawyer or accountant really different to the other? Is it this competitive spirit which gives the poor prospects so much heartache in making up their little minds (see Chapter 9).

Q11   How do you go about assessing pitches?

A11   A massive 62 per cent admitted to adhering to specific criteria, but had no assessment sheet. The remainder did so.

QB'S ASSESSMENT

The fact that all those questioned claimed to have 'specific criteria' for judging a pitch, but only 38 per cent had these criteria laid down on some sort of form against which suppliers were assessed, seems odd to me. If you don't have a form (62 per cent didn't), how casual must your criteria be? Pretty casual, I'd say.

But then, on the other hand, I don't believe forms serve any purpose – throw them in the bin, I say. All they will do is make what is in reality an intuitive decision, into a bureaucratic one. I think that's actually what most of the 62 per cent of the respondents really inwardly believe – but haven't owned up to in themselves. Instead, they weakly claim to have some sort of unnamed specific criteria.

I can accept (although not agree with) the 38 per cent who do employ the assessment form method. But what of the rest? Why don't they admit they base their decision on intangibles, like personal chemistry? See below.

Q12   Rate in importance (10 = high) the specific criteria used when assessing competitive pitches. (See Figure 15)

A12   Unexpectedly, quality scores top – both in terms of people and pitch content (9.1 each). People also come next (8.8) in terms of those who will work 'on your business', and half-way up the table (8.0) in terms of 'people personality'. Interestingly, 'reputation of the company' comes low down in this table (6.6), and 'use of humour' comes last of all (5.1).

QB'S ASSESSMENT

Funny, isn't it, how *people* figure so strongly all of a sudden? My feeling is that 'form-filling' (see item 11) and 'people' don't mix.

The truth, in my view, is that people chemistry – although not articulated in forms, or even verbally for that matter – is the basic key to business success. That apart, it's intesting that the quality/content of the pitch (9.1) dominates over the quality of physical presentation

10 = extremely important	
	Average rating
Quality of content	9.1
Quality/experience of people who will work on the account	9.1
The people pitching will work on your business	8.8
Understanding of your business/market	8.4
Personality of the people	8.0
Quality of physical presentation	6.8
Reputation of the company	6.6
An approach which is not too pushy	6.2
Use of humour	5.1

Source: The Quentin Bell Organisation plc

Figure 15 Average ratings of importance of specific criteria when assessing competitive pitches.

(6.8), although I'm sure anything less than a competent presentation would mark the team down, whether this is articulated by our sample or not. Who wants the embarrassment of a crass performance, with slides upside down and in the wrong order?

As I argued in Chapter 2, 'understanding of your business/market' comes high (8.4), although not as high as I would have expected. Perhaps this speaks even more highly for the importance of the 'quality people issue' (and content) that comes before it.

Finally, why is humour last? I think it's simply because humour is only fun when it *is*, if you follow me. In other words, you can't judge humour hypothetically or in isolation. But, if a pitcher is genuinely witty (as opposed to telling jokes – see Chapter 5) then, in context, it's funny. Otherwise, is this bad news? Must business be serious, rather than amusing, I wonder? You *can* combine humour with a seriousness, I believe – but few manage it as a constant, winning mixture.

Q13 How important are visual aids, and as a prospect, which ones do you prefer?

A13 The majority (52 per cent) believe visual aids to be quite important, with 38 per cent feeling them to be *very* important (a massive 90 per cent between them). OHP is the most preferred support technique (52 per cent), video second (31 per cent), multi-media third (28 per cent) and slides fourth (21 per cent). Charts and display boards come last.

QB'S ASSESSMENT

The fact that 90 per cent believe that visual aids are 'very' or 'quite' important says it all. Doing it without them is like driving without a car – it defies any sense.

Amazingly, the old-fashioned OHP comes top, despite all the hype about computerised techniques (see Top Tip Number 12, Chapter 7), and notwithstanding the fact that multi-media comes third.

Could that be because OHP is the most adaptable, simple technique to use – or is it a self-fulfilling prophecy, in the sense that the more it's used, the more it's wanted? Both, probably.

I'm surprised that video rates so highly, given its lack of flexibility – you can't change the content, as with OHP – or slides, of course, which come surprisingly low down, as do charts and display boards.

But we have to remember that we are seeing this from the prospect's perspective. As pitchers, we would see the practical problems involved. From Mr or Ms Prospect's point of view, a video will look best on the day, despite its inappropriateness for us as the prime movers. See below.

Q14 Which are the most frequently used visual aids? (As opposed to those *preferred* by prospects.)

A14 OHP is still top of the pops (52 per cent) but this time slides and charts (41 per cent and 35 per cent respectively) beat video into fourth place. Multi-media comes next to last, with 21 per cent.

QB'S ASSESSMENT

Well, that's the spice of life in action. So, ladies and gentlemen, whilst our respected clients prefer the high-fallutin' pitch techniques – 31 per cent prefer video and 28 per cent prefer multi-media in question 13 – these pitch tools fall by 3 per cent to 28 per cent (video) and 7 per cent (multi-media) in our 'users' chart (ie those doing the pitching and able to choose their support visuals techniques).

Conversely, old-fashioned but reliable, controllable and simple methods like slides (up a massive 20 per cent) and charts (up a spectacular 21 per cent) are the chosen techniques by suppliers as evidenced by our sample.

So what's the message? It's clear and straightforward, and a good way to finish this book. The message is that it seems the sophisticated high-technology visual techniques are about to follow the fate of the dodo and be consigned to the pitch-bin even before their puberty (the techniques, not the dodo).

Pitchers prefer simple methods, it seems. This may change in time, of course – but only as this new technology itself becomes 'simple', because our new generation of pitchers will have grown up with it (eg my teenaged daughters).

But as things stand today – and leading up to the turn of the century – my prediction is that the simplicity and flexibility of charts, slides and the winning OHP will still dominate. And to me that is damned heartening news, because it means the discriminating factor in winning a pitch, as I've said all along, is not characterised by the physical execution made possible by a wonderous machine. It is characterised by people.

REPRISE

And so we've travelled full circle: the veritable round trip of the pitch, right back to the very first chapter of all and my first two Fundamental Truths.

Do you need reminding? The first says that pitchers are not born, they are made. The second bears repeating:

■■■

People buy people, not organisations. So remember, whilst the reputation of your company and the standard of your physical execution will influence a decision, it will be *you* (and your colleagues) that matter most in clinching the deal.

■■■

Good luck!

INDEX